Teaching Self-Defense in Secondary Physical Education

Joan L. Neide, EdD

Library of Congress Cataloging-in-Publication Data

Neide, Joan.
   Teaching self-defense in secondary physical education / Joan Neide.
      p. cm.
   ISBN-13: 978-0-7360-7486-5 (soft cover)
   ISBN-10: 0-7360-7486-4 (soft cover)
   1. Self-defense--Study and teaching (Secondary)--United States. I. Title.
   GV1111.N4533 2009
   613.6'6--dc22

                              2008032829

ISBN-10: 0-7360-7486-4
ISBN-13: 978-0-7360-7486-5

The Web addresses cited in this text were current as of September 2008, unless otherwise noted.

Acquisitions Editor: Scott Wikgren; **Developmental Editor:** Ragen E. Sanner; **Assistant Editor:** Anne Rumery; **Copyeditor:** Joy Wotherspoon; **Proofreader:** Jim Burns; **Permission Manager:** Dalene Reeder; **Graphic Designer:** Joe Buck; **Graphic Artist:** Yvonne Griffith; **Cover Designer:** Keith Blomberg; **Photographer (cover and interior):** Neil Bernstein; **Photo Production Manager:** Jason Allen, **Art Manager:** Kelly Hendren; **Associate Art Manager:** Alan L. Wilborn; **Illustrator:** Kelly Hendren; **Printer:** Versa Press

Printed in the United States of America   10 9 8 7 6 5 4 3 2 1

Human Kinetics
Web site: www.HumanKinetics.com

United States: Human Kinetics
P.O. Box 5076
Champaign, IL 61825-5076
800-747-4457
e-mail: humank@hkusa.com

Canada: Human Kinetics
475 Devonshire Road Unit 100
Windsor, ON N8Y 2L5
800-465-7301 (in Canada only)
e-mail: info@hkcanada.com

Europe: Human Kinetics
107 Bradford Road
Stanningley
Leeds LS28 6AT, United Kingdom
+44 (0) 113 255 5665
e-mail: hk@hkeurope.com

Australia: Human Kinetics
57A Price Avenue
Lower Mitcham, South Australia 5062
08 8372 0999
e-mail: info@hkaustralia.com

New Zealand: Human Kinetics
Division of Sports Distributors NZ Ltd.
P.O. Box 300 226 Albany
North Shore City
Auckland
0064 9 448 1207
e-mail: info@humankinetics.co.nz

Teaching Self-Defense in Secondary Physical Education

Joan L. Neide, EdD

Human Kinetics

Contents

Part III Releases 53

Part IV Activities and Handouts . . 75

Lesson Finder

This tool will help you to identify and find the materials that go with each lesson. Plans for two- and four-week units are included.

PLAN FOR A TWO-WEEK UNIT

The first two weeks (days 1 to 10) of the self-defense course are a single unit. Students will be introduced to the fundamental physical skills needed to deter an attack, to the principles of home safety, and to the basic facts about and resources for sexual assault. If the sexual assault lessons are not suitable for your school setting, you may substitute lessons on fire and Internet safety.

PLAN FOR A FOUR-WEEK UNIT

During the second two weeks (days 11 to 20), you will continue drilling the students in basic physical skills, but begin teaching them more release techniques. You will also introduce them to the concepts of gender stereotyping, acquaintance rape, the legal aspects of self-defense, and methods for conflict deescalation. Alternative lessons are available if your school determines that lessons dealing with sexual assault are not appropriate.

Day	Skill	Release	Activity	
			Title	Handout
Two-Week Unit				
Day 1	*Teach* • Defensive stance, evasive step, and safety yell, page 32 • Knee kick, page 35		• Introductory Lesson: Self-Defense Questionnaire, page 76 *Alternative* • Fun Beginning: Identifying Ways People Commit Crimes, page 81 • Design an Ad Campaign for School Safety, page 82	• Self-Defense Questionnaire, page 78 • Permission slip, if applicable, page 4 *Alternative* • Crime-Prevention Tips, page 79
Day 2	*Teach* • Front kick, page 37 *Review* • Defensive stance, evasive step, and safety yell, page 32 • Knee kick, page 35			
Day 3	*Teach* • Horse stance, page 34 • Side kick, page 39 • Front and reverse punches, page 43 *Review* • Defensive stance, evasive step, and safety yell, page 32 • Front kick, page 37			

(continued)

Day	Skill	Release	Activity	
			Title	Handout
Two-Week Unit				
Day 4	*Teach* • Heel-of-palm strike, page 45 *Review* • Horse stance, page 34 • Front kick, page 37 • Side kick, page 39 • Front and reverse punches, page 43		• Home Safety: Note-Taking Activity, page 83	• Home Safety, page 86
Day 5	*Review* • Front kick, page 37 • Side kick, page 39 • Front and reverse punches, page 43 • Heel-of-palm strike, page 45		• Contact Points, page 99	• Contact Points, page 101
Day 6	*Teach* • Back fist strike, page 47 • Elbow strikes, page 49 *Review* • Defensive stance, evasive step, and safety yell, page 32	*Teach* • Wrist releases from single, double, and two-handed grabs, page 54		
Day 7			• Myths and Facts About Rape: What Should I Do?, page 106 *Alternative* • Escaping From a House Fire, page 88	• Myths and Facts About Rape, page 108 *Alternative* • Is Your House Safe From Fire?, page 90
Day 8	*Teach* • Back kick, page 41 *Review* • Defensive stance, evasive step, and safety yell, page 32	*Teach* • Full nelson 1, page 64		
Day 9	*Review* • Front kick, page 37 • Side kick, page 39 • Back kick, page 41 • Front and reverse punches, page 43 • Heel-of-palm strike, page 45 • Back fist strike, page 47 • Elbow strikes, page 49		• Stages of Acquaintance Rape, page 118 *Alternative* • Internet Safety, page 91	• Scenario for Stages of Acquaintance Rape, page 120 • Self-Defense Individual Skills Test, page 16 *Alternative* • Internet Safety, page 94
Day 10			• Self-Defense Scenarios, page 102	• Self-Defense Scenarios: Two-Week Unit (10 days), page 104 • Individual Release Assessment, page 18

Day	Skill	Release	Activity	
			Title	Handout
Four-Week Unit				
Day 11	*Review* • Front and reverse punches, page 43 • Heel-of-palm strike, page 45 • Back fist strike, page 47		*Review* • Contact Points, page 99	
Day 12			• Acquaintance Rape and Gender Stereotyping, page 113 *Alternative* • Knowing Your Rights and Trusting Your Feelings, page 124	• Acquaintance Rape Story, page 117
Day 13	*Review* • Defensive stance, evasive step, and safety yell, page 32 • Horse stance, page 34 • Knee kick, page 35 • Front kick, page 37 • Back kick, page 41 • Front and reverse punches, page 43 • Heel-of-palm strike, page 45	*Teach* • Full nelson 2, page 66 • Head hold, page 68 *Review* • Full nelson 1, page 64		
Day 14	*Review* • Defensive stance, evasive step, and safety yell, page 32 • Horse stance, page 34 • Knee kick, page 35 • Front kick, page 37 • Side kick, page 39 • Back kick, page 41 • Elbow strikes, page 49	*Teach* • Rear bear hug 1, page 58 • Rear bear hug 2, page 60 • Front bear hug, page 62		
Day 15			• Deescalating a Potential Confrontation, page 95	• Deescalation Task Sheets, pages 96-98
Day 16	*Review* • Elbow strikes, page 49	*Review* • Full nelson 1, page 64 • Full nelson 2, page 66 • Head hold, page 68		• Crime-Prevention Tips, page 79
Day 17		*Teach* • Front choke, page 70 • Rear choke, page 72		
Days 18 and 19			• Self-Defense Scenarios, page 102	• Self-Defense Scenarios: Four-Week Unit (20 days), page 105
Day 20			• Legal Aspects of Self-Defense, page 121	• You Be the Judge, page 123

Preface

Self-defense is a system of mental preparation and defensive tactics that helps people develop the poise and confidence to handle threatening situations effectively and with minimal confrontation. The lessons presented are simple, effective, and practical. They are appropriate for a coed physical education class during a 50- to 60-minute class period. This manual contains specific, practical strategies and lessons that can be used for any physical education setting. Physical education instructors are encouraged to be creative in adapting units that are appropriate for their students. The main objectives in every self-defense unit should be simplicity, effectiveness, and conflict avoidance.

So, what should a two- or four-week self-defense unit in a secondary physical education program address? This book's eclectic approach begins with tactics and techniques from martial art systems, combatives such as wrestling, and police and military organizations. It combines these skills with common sense, a basic presentation of home and personal safety, and the principle of minimal confrontation.

The lessons ask students to think critically about their homes and personal safety practices and to make sound decisions that will minimize opportunities for them to be victimized. Students will learn the necessary motor skills and movement patterns for a variety of self-defense techniques. They will participate and cooperate with their peers in a challenging setting that has practical meaning and will define their own limitations in regard to self-defense. The overall goal, however, is to help students gain the confidence and poise to effectively cope with and react to potentially dangerous situations.

Introduction

Teaching Self-Defense in Secondary Physical Education provides a practical and appropriate approach to teaching self-defense in a physical education class. The lessons are designed to accommodate large coed classes during time frames of 50 to 60 minutes, but they can easily be expanded or reduced to accommodate other class lengths. The manual introduces lesson plans for two- and four-week self-defense units. You can choose from a variety of activities, skills, and releases to design a unit appropriate for the needs of your students and the facilities and equipment available at your school. The units and their accompanying instructions are listed in a sequential format that is easy to follow.

PLANNING THE UNIT

When you plan the unit and its lessons, your main concern must be safety. The self-defense skills and releases in this book deter attacks. Therefore, it is possible for students to be injured during instruction. It is advisable to adhere to the following safety precautions:

1. Students will be required to wear clothing that is appropriate for an active physical education class.
2. Students may not wear jewelry on physically active days.
3. Students will learn and consistently review the safety precautions necessary for each skill.
4. Students will choose their partners in order to create a learning environment that is emotionally and physically safe.
5. Unless otherwise specified, students will perform all techniques slowly and carefully. Safety will always be the main objective.
6. Students will never perform a technique with an open hand near a partner's eyes.
7. Students will be cautious when practicing kicks, especially those aimed at the knees and groin.
8. The instructor will monitor the class at all times and will not allow students to work independently unless they all understand the instructions and safety precautions for a specific task.
9. The instructor will be aware of students' physical limitations and should be prepared to adapt tasks for individual needs.

Goals

The key to developing self-defense units of high quality is to set goals that can be realistically accomplished during two or four weeks of instruction. According to Rink (2006), physical education has the potential to contribute to educational goals and objectives in all learning domains. The self-defense unit contributes to these goals through active learning and physical activity. Students will be asked to think critically about their homes and personal safety practices, and to make sound decisions that will minimize opportunities for them to be victimized. They will also learn the basic physical skills for handling an assailant with minimal confrontation. The following outline lists realistic goals for a two-week unit.

Students will be able to do the following:

1. Define their limitations in respect to self-defense.
2. Display a level of confidence and poise necessary to cope with and react to potentially dangerous situations.
3. Identify a variety of security precautions for situations in and outside of the home.
4. Identify the medical and legal procedures related to sexual and violent assaults.
5. Demonstrate the basic physical skills and releases required for handling an assailant with minimal confrontation.
6. Display acceptance and respect for classmates with varying skill levels.

The following outline lists realistic goals for a four-week unit.
Students will be able to do the following:

1. Display a level of confidence and poise necessary to effectively cope with and react to potentially dangerous situations.
2. Define their limitations in regard to self-defense.
3. Identify security precautions for situations in and outside of the home.
4. Identify the legal aspects of personal defense.
5. Identify the medical and legal procedures related to sexual and violent assaults.
6. Demonstrate the basic physical skills and releases required for handling an assailant with minimal confrontation.
7. Demonstrate overall improvement in areas of physical fitness, including strength, endurance, flexibility, and coordination.
8. Display acceptance and respect for classmates of varying skill levels.

Assessment

Assessment is an important factor to consider when designing a self-defense unit. According to Darst and Pangrazi (2006), physical education assessment comes in two forms: formal assessment, which affects grading procedures, and informal assessment, which obtains knowledge about student performance but does not determine grades. This book provides plans for both forms of assessment.

The informal assessment plans for the self-defense units help students solve problems with tools such as task sheets, informational posters, and role-playing activities. Students will integrate and demonstrate the principles of self-defense with formal assessment tools such as question-and-answer sheets, homework assignments, and a written test (see appendix). Finally, students will explain and demonstrate practical applications for the skills and releases they have learned through self-defense scenarios. See days 9 and 10 for sample rubrics. With this system, you can assign grades for students based on specific goals and objectives. You should choose an assessment plan that fits your needs and integrate it into the unit.

LESSON PLANS

Part I of the manual outlines lesson plans for 20 days of instruction. The subsequent parts of the book provide supplemental information on activities, skills, and releases. The first two weeks of the self-defense course serve as a single unit. Students will learn the fundamental physical skills needed to deter an attack, preventive measures for home safety, and basic facts about and resources for sexual assault.

In the second two weeks, you will review basic physical skills, teach more release techniques, and introduce students to the concepts of gender stereotyping, acquaintance rape, legal aspects of self-defense, and methods for conflict deescalation. If you have time, you may include lesson plans that explore fire and Internet safety.

If your school determines that sexual assault lessons are not appropriate for your setting, you can substitute the following lessons:

Escaping From a House Fire

Internet Safety

Knowing Your Rights and Trusting Your Feelings

Warm-Ups

Although each lesson plan designates time to warm up before physical activity, this book does not describe specific warm-ups. Secondary physical education classes typically already have a prescribed warm-up routine. All lessons are compatible with both established warm-up routines or a warm-up specific to self-defense skills created by you.

A self-defense warm-up can begin with a cardiorespiratory warm-up routine using the evasive step (see Defensive Stance, Evasive Step, and Safety Yell, page 32), which guides students in movements from side to side. As the students learn more techniques, you can add kicks (see Knee Kick, page 35; Front Kick, page 37; Side Kick, page 39; and Back Kick, page 41) and punches (see Front and Reverse Punches, page 43; and Back Fist Strike, page 47) to the evasive stepping. You can follow this exercise by asking students to maintain a defensive stance and perform repetitive kicks or hand techniques to a cadence. You may vary the routine by asking the students to alternate punches from a horse stance (see Horse Stance, page 34). Be creative. Follow all warm-ups with a series of exercises that safely stretch all muscle groups.

Activities

This section of the manual presents 14 activities that can be used in either two- or four-week units. Determine which activities are appropriate for the size and maturity level of your class. The activities are based on active learning strategies. Active learning, a unique teaching style, can help invigorate your students to use higher-order-thinking tasks, such as analysis, synthesis, and evaluation. Here is Silberman's (1996) description:

> " Active learning of information, skills, and attitudes occurs through a process of inquiry. Students are in a searching mode rather than a reactive mode. That is, they are looking for answers to questions either posed to them or posed by them. They are seeking solutions to problems teachers have challenged them to solve. They are interested in obtaining information or skills to complete tasks assigned to them. And they are confronted with issues that compel them to examine what they believe and value (67). "

The activities you can use in the classroom or gymnasium to foster active learning are endless. Remember that active learning strategies require students to talk, listen, write, read, and reflect. Students are challenged to find solutions to problems and to apply what they have learned. Active learning should be fun, fast-paced, and directed and supported by the teacher. Ask your students to take responsibility for their own learning, and let the excitement of education begin.

Skills and Releases

The skill and release sections of the manual break down the activity into instructional steps. Rink suggests that skill acquisition begins with identifying the extension aspects of skill development (2006). In other words, the teacher must present the content in a simple format, and structure the lesson to create a sequence, or chain, of experiences. All skills and releases presented in this manual are segmented into a sequential learning event. As you modify the lessons for your class, remember to

- practice the parts,
- focus the intent of the performance,
- change the conditions of the performance,
- add or decrease the number of combined skills or actions, and
- expand the number of responses.

Good teaching helps students to refine their skills. According to Fronske, motor-learning specialists have long noted that simple instructions help students concentrate on the skill at hand, and cues serve as a guide to suggest or stimulate their imagination to action (2008). Each skill and release lesson provides teaching cues that will help your students concentrate on the technique.

Avoidance, however, is the first line of self-defense. Realistically, many of the skills and techniques in this book will not be 100% successful. Students should be aware that they may not be able to adequately defend themselves in every situation. The main goal of your self-defense unit is to give each student the confidence to say, "No," the poise to deescalate a situation, and the knowledge to prevent or deter a crime.

REFERENCES

Darst, P., and R. Pangrazi. 2006. *Dynamic Physical Education for Secondary School Students*. San Francisco, CA: Pearson Benjamin Cummings.

Fronske, H. 2008. *Teaching Cues for Sport Skills for Secondary School Students*. 4th ed. San Francisco, CA: Pearson Education.

Rink, J. 2006. *Teaching Physical Education for Learning*. 5th ed. New York: McGraw Hill.

Silberman, M. 1996. *Active Learning 101: Strategies to Teach Any Subject*. MA: Allyn & Bacon.

Part 1

Lesson Plans

Day 1

Day	Skill	Release	Activity	
			Title	**Handout**
Day 1	*Teach* • Defensive stance, evasive step, and safety yell, page 32 • Knee kick, page 35		• Introductory Lesson: Self-Defense Questionnaire, page 76 *Alternative* • Fun Beginning: Identifying Ways People Commit Crimes, page 81 • Design an Ad Campaign for School Safety, page 82	• Self-Defense Questionnaire, page 78 • Permission slip, if applicable, page 4 *Alternative* • Crime-Prevention Tips, page 79

Objectives

Students will be able to do the following:

1. Complete the self-defense questionnaire and discuss the answers at the end of the activity.
2. Demonstrate a defensive stance and evasive step during drills.
3. Demonstrate a safety yell while performing a knee kick.
4. Identify when and why the safety yell should be used.
5. Demonstrate an effective knee kick with a partner.
6. Cooperate with a partner, adhering to all safety rules.

Equipment and Facilities

▶ Gym
▶ Handout: Self-Defense Questionnaire, page 78
▶ Overhead projector
▶ Permission slip (see sample on page 4 or use one specific to your school or school district)

Warm-Ups

Begin with a cardiorespiratory warm-up and follow with a series of exercises that safely stretch all major muscle groups.

Procedure

1. Hand out the Self-Defense Questionnaire to the students.
2. Assign small groups for discussion or ask students to work on the questions with a partner. When the class is finished, ask various students to read each question aloud and obtain their opinions on the correct answer.
3. Explain all the safety rules that will be used in the class. Emphasize that all techniques will be done in a safe, nonthreatening environment and that physical force is the last resort in self-defense. Make students aware that avoidance and common sense are crucial to self-defense.
4. Introduce the defensive stance and evasive step.

5. Demonstrate the safety yell and identify when and why to use it.
6. Demonstrate the knee kick and ask students to practice it, both alone and with a partner.

Conclusion

Ask students to identify the proper steps for executing a knee kick and the critical elements of a defensive stance and a safety yell. Explain that the main focus of the self-defense unit is awareness and avoidance. A portion of the unit, however, will address sexual assault. In order to participate in this portion of the unit, students need permission from a parent or guardian. Hand out permission slips to each student to be returned by the next class.

Note: If you will be substituting alternative lessons for sexual assault topics, you will not need to distribute permission slips.

Permission Slip

Dear parents or guardians:

Your child is participating in a self-defense unit through the school's physical education program. The focus of this self-defense unit is awareness and avoidance. Students will be asked to think critically about their homes and sense of personal safety and to learn the basic physical skills required to handle an attacker with minimal confrontation.

A portion of this unit will address sexual assault. The information provided to students will be age appropriate and will focus on avoidance. The following is a list of discussion topics that will be taught in this unit:

- ▶ Socialization: gender stereotyping
- ▶ Identifying possible situations for assault or rape
- ▶ Myths and facts about rape
- ▶ Support services

If you agree that your child may participate in the classes on sexual assault, please check the space next to the corresponding statement below and sign the slip.

If you do not give your permission, please check the space next to the corresponding statement below and sign the slip. Your child will receive alternative assignments.

Thank you.

- -

Child's name _____ Date _____

_____ Yes, my child may participate in the classes addressing sexual assault.

_____ No, I do not want my child to participate in the sexual assault classes and understand that he or she will be given an alternative assignment.

_____

Parent or guardian signature

From J. Neide, 2009, Teaching Self-Defense in Secondary Physical Education (Champaign, IL: Human Kinetics).

Day 2

Day	Skill	Release	Activity	
			Title	Handout
Day 2	*Teach* • Front kick, page 37 *Review* • Defensive stance, evasive step, and safety yell, page 32 • Knee kick, page 35			

Objectives

Students will be able to do the following:

1. Execute and practice the defensive stance, evasive step, and safety yell during drills.
2. Demonstrate the technique for an effective knee kick with a partner.
3. Execute an effective front kick from a defensive stance.
4. Identify the contact points used in the front kick and knee kick.
5. Adhere to all safety procedures during drills and applications.

Equipment and Facilities

▶ Gym
▶ Folding panel mats
▶ Kicking shields (optional)

Warm-Ups

Begin with a cardiorespiratory warm-up and follow with a series of exercises that safely stretch all major muscle groups.

Procedure

1. Collect permission slips from the previous lesson, if applicable.
2. Review the defensive stance and evasive step. Ask students to face each other and practice moving toward and away from their partners. Partners should feel comfortable working together during the drill.
3. Review knee kick. Students should stay with their original partners and follow all safety procedures while practicing the knee kick. One student acts as the assailant, and the other as the target. The assailant places hands on the target's shoulder. The target should perform the knee kick and move away into a defensive stance. Encourage the students to use a safety yell on knee impact. Emphasize that all techniques are done slowly and without force or contact. Watch the students for good form and balance.
4. Demonstrate the front kick. Ask students to line up and perform the kick following your cadence.

5. If time permits, students may practice kicking a folded panel mat. Ask one or two students to hold the mat vertically. Students must kick slowly in the beginning, making contact with either their toes, balls of their feet, or heels.

Conclusion

Bring the students together and go over the class safety rules. Have the students identify the targeted contact points of the front kick.

Day 3

Day	Skill	Release	Activity	
			Title	Handout
Day 3	*Teach* • Horse stance, page 34 • Side kick, page 39 • Front and reverse punches, page 43 *Review* • Defensive stance, evasive step, and safety yell, page 32 • Front kick, page 37			

Objectives

Students will be able to do the following:

1. Demonstrate and drill the front kick using the toes, ball of the foot, and heel.
2. Execute the side kick with a partner, using the knife edge of the foot and adhering to all safety rules.
3. Demonstrate proper form for the front and reverse punches during drills.
4. Execute the front and reverse punches from the defensive stance, both following the teacher's cadence and with a partner during drills.
5. Perform the horse stance and demonstrate full punches from this position following the teacher's cadence.
6. Identify the targeted vital areas used by the front kick, knee kick, and side kick.

Equipment and Facilities

▶ Gym
▶ 8.5-by-11-inch (22 by 28 cm) sheets of paper

Warm-Ups

Begin with a cardiorespiratory warm-up and follow with a series of exercises that safely stretch all major muscle groups. Cardiorespiratory warm-ups can include moving back and forth using the evasive step.

Procedure

1. Introduce the front and reverse punches, paying particular attention to the fist position and the roll of the arm. Ask the class to perform front punches from the defensive stance. They may complete a set of reverse punches followed by front punches or perform each punch individually. Encourage the students to be strong. Students can use a safety yell on each punch or on the 10th punch.
2. Students should maintain a defensive stance and perform front kicks following a cadence. Variation: Students can perform a reverse punch and follow with a kick with the back leg.
3. Introduce the side kick and drill each part of the kick, watching for good form and posture. Identify the knee as the target area. Review the safety procedure for working with partners. Ask students to drill with partners if time permits.

4. Introduce the horse stance and end the class by asking students to perform alternating punches from the horse stance position.

Conclusion

Ask the students to identify the key elements of a successful side kick and punch. Emphasize that incorrect form in any of the physical skills can cause injury if they actually make contact with a surface. Using an incorrect fist position can cause finger fracture or wrist injury. Similarly, incorrect ankle position during a kick can cause injury to the ankle and toes. Students should direct front kicks to the groin area and side kicks to the knee while being careful to avoid making contact.

Day 4

Day	Skill	Release	Activity	
			Title	Handout
Day 4	*Teach* • Heel-of-palm strike, page 45 *Review* • Horse stance, page 34 • Front kick, page 37 • Side kick, page 39 • Front and reverse punches, page 43		• Home Safety, page 83	• Home Safety, page 86

Objectives

Students will be able to do the following:

1. Recognize how to make their homes secure and how to feel personally safe outside of the home.
2. Take notes on the key components of home safety during lecture.
3. Demonstrate the heel-of-palm strike and identify the vital target areas for this technique.
4. Execute the front kick, side kick, and punches during cadenced drills.

Equipment and Facilities

▶ Gym
▶ Handout: Home Safety, page 86
▶ Pencils
▶ Overhead projector

Warm-Ups

Begin with a cardiorespiratory warm-up and follow with a series of exercises that safely stretch all major muscle groups.

Procedure

1. Create a lecture-based discussion on home safety. Ask students to complete the handout and answer any questions they might have about the lecture.
2. Introduce the heel-of-palm strike and lead drills from the defensive stance. Emphasize that the nose is the target for this technique. The nose is structurally weakest on the sides, so a side hit will cause the greatest damage, but a frontal hit can also be very effective and painful. When struck on the nose, the assailant's eyes will tear up and momentarily lose vision. This partial loss of vision will give the intended target a chance to escape.
3. Finish by drilling front kicks and side kicks from the defensive stance. Follow this exercise with punches from the horse stance.

Conclusion

Summarize the main points of home safety.

Day 5

Day	Skill	Release	Activity	
			Title	Handout
Day 5	*Review* • Front kick, page 37 • Side kick, page 39 • Front and reverse punches, page 43 • Heel-of-palm strike, page 45		• Contact Points, page 99	• Contact Points, page 101

Objectives

Students will be able to do the following:

1. Create a figure drawing and identify contact points that are used with self-defense techniques.
2. Describe the level of damage that can occur in self-defense and the consequences of using physical force.
3. Acknowledge their limitations while performing a variety of physical techniques.
4. Execute the front kick, side kick, heel-of-palm strike, and front and reverse punches, following the teacher's cadence during drills.

Equipment and Facilities

▶ Gym
▶ 3-by-6-foot (1 by 2 m) sheet of paper for each group
▶ Markers
▶ Tape
▶ Anatomical chart (optional)

Warm-Ups

Begin with a cardiorespiratory warm-up and follow with a series of exercises that safely stretch all major muscle groups.

Procedure

1. Create a lecture-based discussion on contact points. Discuss traumas that can occur during self-defense and proper techniques.
2. Ask the students to form groups, trace their bodies on paper, and mark the contact points. Hang the drawings on the wall and ask the students to demonstrate the front kick, side kick, front and reverse punches, and heel-of-palm strikes to the contact points. The students can add a safety yell when they perform the techniques. If time permits, you can direct the students to slowly and carefully practice the techniques with partners. Ask the students to perform the drill at your count when aiming their strikes at a partner. You must enforce all safety precautions during this activity.

3. Conclude by drilling the previously learned skills to a cadence. Students should practice drills from the horse stance or the defensive stance.

Conclusion

Summarize the contact points and the potential for damage to each area during self-defense. The level of damage depends on the force, angle of attack, method, and hitting technique used, as well as the composition of the assailant's body. Discuss student limitations, such as weight, strength, and height.

Day 6

Day	Skill	Release	Activity	
			Title	Handout
Day 6	*Teach* • Back fist strike, page 47 • Elbow strikes, page 49 *Review* • Defensive stance, evasive step, and safety yell, page 32	*Teach* • Wrist releases from single, double, and two-handed grabs, page 54		

Objectives

Students will be able to do the following:

1. Execute a proper back fist strike from a defensive stance.
2. Identify the key contact point for the back fist strike.
3. Cooperate with a partner during the paper drill.
4. Execute and drill the front, side, and back elbow strikes following the teacher's cadence.
5. Demonstrate and drill the wrist release from a single, double, and two-handed grab with a partner.
6. Cooperate with their partners, adhering to all safety rules.

Equipment and Facilities

▶ Gym
▶ 8.5-by-11-inch (22 by 28 cm) sheets of paper

Warm-Ups

Begin with a cardiorespiratory warm-up and follow with a series of exercises that safely stretch all major muscle groups.

Procedure

1. Introduce the elbow strikes. Drill the technique from a good defensive stance and emphasize the aiming points.
2. Introduce the back fist strike to the students and then ask them to drill the exercise with a partner holding a piece of paper.
3. Demonstrate a wrist release from a single, double, and two-handed grab, and ask students to practice these techniques.
4. Create several scenarios in which students are grabbed by an assailant and they must perform a back fist or elbow strike before attempting the wrist release. Check their execution for use of good balance, proper form, and safety precautions (see Variations, pages 56-57).

Conclusion

Review safety procedures with the students. Emphasize that they should use a hand or foot technique before attempting a release. Ask them to identify the key contact point for a back fist strike.

Day 7

Day	Skill	Release	Activity	
			Title	Handout
Day 7			• Myths and Facts About Rape, page 106 *Alternative* • Escaping From a House Fire, page 88	• Myths and Facts About Rape, page 108 *Alternative* • Is Your House Safe From Fire?, page 90

Objectives

Students will be able to do the following:

1. Identify the main facts about sexual assault.
2. Participate in a discussion on sexual assault.
3. Identify the steps to take if they are sexually assaulted and how to help a friend who has been assaulted.

Equipment and Facilities

▶ Classroom
▶ Handout: Myths and Facts About Rape, page 108
▶ Overhead projector
▶ 3-by-5-inch (8 by 13 cm) cards (optional)

Procedure

1. Provide a questionnaire on the myths and facts about rape that is appropriate for the age and maturity levels of the class.
2. Ask the students to complete the handout and to think about questions that they would like to have answered. Because sexual assault is a very sensitive subject, many students will not want to ask a question publicly. You can provide 3-by-5-inch (8 by 13 cm) cards for students to write down their questions privately.
3. After students complete the handout, answer their questions using overhead transparencies (see pages 111 and 112). Review the procedure they should take if a rape occurs.

Conclusion

Use this time as an open question-and-answer time.

Day 8

Day	Skill	Release	Activity	
			Title	Handout
Day 8	*Teach* • Back kick, page 41 *Review* • Defensive stance, evasive step, and safety yell, page 32	*Teach* • Full nelson 1, page 64		

Objectives

Students will be able to do the following:

1. Demonstrate the ability to say, *"No!"* with a partner.
2. Demonstrate a safety yell and identify appropriate times to use it.
3. Execute a back kick from standing and kneeling positions with a partner.
4. Demonstrate the full nelson release 1.
5. Work cooperatively with a partner, adhering to all safety rules.
6. Review the home and personal safety tips.
7. Display personal confidence.

Equipment and Facilities

▶ Gym
▶ Floor mats
▶ Folded panel mats (optional)
▶ Kicking shields (optional)

Warm-Ups

Begin with a cardiorespiratory warm-up and follow with a series of exercises that safely stretch all major muscle groups.

Procedure

1. Begin the lesson by demonstrating assertive body language and verbal communication. Remind students that, for a crime to occur, assailants must have the desire, the ability, and the opportunity. Students can decrease an assailant's opportunity or desire to commit a crime by being confident and assertive.
2. Introduce and drill the back kick and the kneeling variation. If you have time, ask students to practice kicking into folded panel mats or kicking shields.
3. Introduce the full nelson release, emphasizing the importance of staying loose and agile. Ask students to practice the technique with partners, both with and without the back kick. Emphasize maintaining a safe distance from their partner when performing the back kick.

Conclusion

Review the three elements assailants need to commit a crime. Summarize the key points of protecting themselves and their homes, avoiding conflict, and displaying confidence.

Day 9

Day	Skill	Release	Activity	
			Title	**Handout**
Day 9	*Review* • Front kick, page 37 • Side kick, page 39 • Back kick, page 41 • Front and reverse punches, page 43 • Heel-of-palm strike, page 45 • Back fist strike, page 47 • Elbow strikes, page 49		• Stages of Acquaintance Rape, page 118 *Alternative* • Internet Safety, page 91	• Scenario for Stages of Acquaintance Rape, page 120 • Self-Defense Individual Skills Test, page 16 *Alternative* • Internet Safety, page 94

Objectives

Students will be able to do the following:

1. Identify the stages of acquaintance rape.
2. Strategize about measures that can reduce the risk of sexual assault.

Equipment and Facilities

▶ Gym
▶ Handout: Scenario for Stages of Acquaintance Rape, page 120
▶ Overhead projector

Warm-Ups

Begin with a cardiorespiratory warm-up and follow with a series of exercises that safely stretch all major muscle groups.

Procedure

1. Create a lecture-based discussion on the stages of acquaintance rape.
2. Preassign students to compatible discussion groups to create an environment where students feel comfortable discussing the subject matter. Distribute the handout and ask students to read the story, answer the questions that follow, and discuss their answers in their small groups. Bring the class together to discuss and clarify their answers.
3. Conclude by reviewing the following techniques: front kick, side kick, back kicks, front and reverse punches, back fist strike, heel-of-palm strike, and elbow strikes. You may drill each technique separately or in combinations.

Conclusion

Open the discussion for questions from students.
Note: You can also use this day to assess and grade students' physical skills. Form students into groups and ask them to perform different skills with your cadence. Use the following rubric as an example to grade students' physical skills.

Self-Defense Individual Skills Test

Example

Name _____ Class _____ Final grade _____

Circle no, partial, or yes. You may add comments for more specific feedback.

Skill	Technique and balance			Power and assertiveness			Grade
Front kick with ball of foot	No	Partial	Yes	No	Partial	Yes	
	Comment:			Comment:			
Side kick to knee	No	Partial	Yes	No	Partial	Yes	
	Comment:			Comment:			
Back kick to groin	No	Partial	Yes	No	Partial	Yes	
	Comment:			Comment:			
Upward elbow strike to nose or chin	No	Partial	Yes	No	Partial	Yes	
	Comment:			Comment:			
Back fist strike to nose	No	Partial	Yes	No	Partial	Yes	
	Comment:			Comment:			
Heel-of-palm strike to nose or chin	No	Partial	Yes	No	Partial	Yes	
	Comment:			Comment:			

Grading Procedure

Use the following table to determine a grade for each skill. Add the grades for all the skills performed and average them for the final grade.

Technique and balance	Power and assertiveness	Grade range
Yes	Yes	A
Yes	Partial	B
Partial	Partial	B/C
Yes	No	C
Partial	No	C/D
No	No	F

From J. Neide, 2009, Teaching Self-Defense in Secondary Physical Education (Champaign, IL: Human Kinetics).

Day 10

Day	Skill	Release	Activity	
			Title	Handout
Day 10			• Self-Defense Scenarios, page 102	• Self-Defense Scenarios: Two-Week Unit (10 days), page 104 • Individual Release Assessment Rubric, page 18

Objectives

Students will be able to do the following:

1. Analyze potentially dangerous situations and determine the best course of action.
2. Demonstrate self-defense moves that are practical and efficient for each scenario.
3. Evaluate the effectiveness of their chosen self-defense techniques.

Equipment and Facilities

▶ Gym
▶ Handout: Self-Defense Scenario (two-week unit), page 104
▶ Individual Release Assessment Rubric, page 18
▶ Chairs (optional)
▶ Mats (optional)

Warm-Ups

Begin with a cardiorespiratory warm-up and follow with a series of exercises that safely stretch all major muscle groups.

Procedure

1. Create a list of potentially dangerous scenarios in which students must use self-defense skills to either protect themselves or to defuse the situation.
2. You may either guide the class through the handout, explaining and working through the scenarios one at a time, or distribute the handout and allow the students to work through the scenarios at their own pace.
3. At the end of the class or after each scenario, bring the class together to share their techniques and analyze how the situations might have either been prevented or defused. Emphasize that the best method of self-defense is to avoid conflict. You can assess students' performance with the provided Individual Release Assessment Rubric.

Conclusion

Remind students to defend themselves by using common sense, trusting their instincts, and avoiding conflict whenever possible. They can prevent crimes by developing good habits that deprive criminals of the opportunity to attack.

Individual Release Assessment Rubric

Grade

A. Excellent—A skill in this category means the student chose correct techniques, showed power, maintained good balance, and displayed an assertive attitude.

B. Strong—A skill in this category means the student chose correct techniques and maintained good balance, but showed little power and displayed minimal assertiveness.

C. Adequate—A skill in this category means the student chose correct techniques, but hesitated and may have needed prompting. The student showed some power, maintained good balance, and displayed an acceptable attitude of assertiveness.

D. Poor—A skill in this category means the student performed the technique incorrectly, but showed an acceptable level of power, balance, and assertiveness.

E. Fundamentally deficient—A skill in this category means the student performed the skill incorrectly, and showed no balance, power, or assertiveness.

From J. Neide, 2009, Teaching Self-Defense in Secondary Physical Education (Champaign, IL: Human Kinetics).

Day 11

Day	Skill	Release	Activity	
			Title	Handout
Day 11	*Review* • Front and reverse punches, page 43 • Heel-of-palm strike, page 45 • Back fist strike, page 47		• Contact Points, page 99	

Objectives

Students will be able to do the following:

1. Drill their skills individually or in combination.
2. Demonstrate directing hand and foot attacks to contact points with a partner, adhering to all safety procedures.
3. Evaluate their limitations during drills.

Equipment and Facilities

▶ Gym

▶ 8.5-by-11-inch (22 by 28 cm) sheets of paper

▶ Anatomical chart

Warm-Ups

Begin with a cardiorespiratory warm-up and follow with a series of exercises that safely stretch all major muscle groups.

Procedure

1. Bring an anatomical chart to class to review contact points. Emphasize the weakest parts of the body (see Contact Points, page 99). Remind students that the level of damage during attack depends on the force, angle, method, and hitting technique used, as well as the composition of the assailant's body. Emphasize that different techniques will be effective for each student given his or her unique strengths and limitations. Again, avoidance is the best line of self-defense.

2. Ask the students to form pairs. Each student should slowly and carefully go through the techniques with a partner. Encourage students to experiment with combinations of skills, using the following list as a guide.

   • Eyes: finger strike or thumbs
   • Chin: heel-of-palm strike, forward or reverse punch, elbow strike
   • Nose: heel-of-palm strike, back fist, forward or reverse punch, elbow strike
   • Trachea: finger strike, forward or reverse punch, back fist, choke hold, elbow strike
   • Larynx: finger strike, forward or reverse punch, back fist, choke hold, elbow strike
   • Sternum: forward or reverse punch, elbow strike
   • Solar plexus: forward or reverse punch, elbow strike
   • Genitalia: front kick, back kick, forward or reverse punch

- Knee: front kick, back kick, side kick
- Toe joints: stomp
- Fingers: grab, bend, and twist

3. Ask one student in each pair of partners to hold out a sheet of paper and the other to assume a defensive stance. The active partner should attempt to hit the paper using front and reverse punches, back fists, and heel-of-palm strikes. Students should switch roles so everyone has a chance to practice.

Conclusion

Summarize the vital target areas and remind students to acknowledge their limitations and to use the self-defense techniques that will be the most effective for their body type, height, and weight.

Day 12

Day	Skill	Release	Activity	
			Title	Handout
Day 12			• Acquaintance Rape and Gender Stereotyping, page 113 *Alternative* • Knowing Your Rights and Trusting Your Feelings, page 124	• Acquaintance Rape Story, page 117

Objectives

Students will be able to do the following:

1. Answer and identify key questions about acquaintance rape in a small group scenario assignment.
2. Define gender stereotyping for their society.
3. Cooperate with and listen to their classmates in a very frank discussion on acquaintance rape.

Equipment and Facilities

▶ Gym or classroom
▶ Handout: Acquaintance Rape Story, page 117

Procedure

1. Distribute the Acquaintance Rape Story handout, then ask students to sit and read the story individually. After the students have read the handout, place them in groups to discuss the questions that follow the story. Because the issue of sexual assault is sensitive, you should preassign the discussion groups for compatibility and a feeling of safety. Encourage the students to discuss the questions honestly and maturely.

2. Bring the class together and introduce the term *gender stereotyping* (see Acquaintance Rape and Gender Stereotyping, page 113). Identify places in the story where the portrayal of both the boy's and girl's actions would be considered gender stereotyping.

3. Use the additional information in Acquaintance Rape and Gender Stereotyping to lead a discussion on stereotypical gender roles and preventive measures against rape.

Conclusion

Summarize the main points of gender stereotyping and allow time to answer students' questions.

Day 13

Day	Skill	Release	Activity	
			Title	Handout
Day 13	*Review* • Defensive stance, evasive step, and safety yell, page 32 • Horse stance, page 34 • Knee kick, page 35 • Front kick, page 37 • Back kick, page 41 • Front and reverse punches, page 43 • Heel-of-palm strike, page 45	*Teach* • Full nelson 2, page 66 • Head hold, page 68 *Review* • Full nelson 1, page 64		

Objectives

Students will be able to do the following:

1. Properly execute the full nelson release 1 with a partner.
2. Demonstrate the full nelson release 2 with a partner.
3. Demonstrate a release from a head hold with a partner.
4. Identify the contact points.
5. Cooperate with a partner, adhering to all safety precautions.

Equipment and Facilities

▶ Gym
▶ Mats (optional)

Warm-Ups

Begin with a cardiorespiratory warm-up and follow with a series of exercises that safely stretch all major muscle groups.

Procedure

1. Begin the class with a review of the full nelson release 1. Ask students to choose partners and practice the full nelson release 1 with and without the back kick.
2. Review the basic horse stance in preparation for teaching a variation of the full nelson release.
3. Demonstrate the alternate full nelson release, but emphasize that to successfully execute this technique, students must have a strong upper body and be the same height as or taller than the assailant. Partners should practice each release.
4. Once students have mastered the full nelson release 2, introduce an evasive step after the release. This step puts the student in a good position to next execute a heel-of-palm strike, front and reverse punches, or a front kick.

5. Introduce the release for a head hold. Encourage students to use their free hands and feet as potential weapons before and after the release (see Variations, page 69). Remind them to aim for the most vulnerable areas on the attacker's body: the eyes, knees, and groin.

Conclusion

Discuss the key points of the full nelson releases and the head hold. Remind students to choose releases appropriate for their body type, height, and weight.

Day 14

Day	Skill	Release	Activity	
			Title	Handout
Day 14	*Review* • Defensive stance, evasive step, and safety yell, page 32 • Horse stance, page 34 • Knee kick, page 35 • Front kick, page 37 • Side kick, page 39 • Back kick, page 41 • Elbow strikes, page 49	*Teach* • Rear bear hug 1, page 58 • Rear bear hug 2, page 60 • Front bear hug, page 62		

Objectives

Students will be able to do the following:

1. Demonstrate two different releases from a rear bear hug with a partner.
2. Demonstrate a release from a front bear hug with a partner.
3. Identify and execute strikes to contact points during a release.
4. Work cooperatively with a partner, adhering to all safety precautions.
5. Identify kicks that can serve as a prerelease attack.

Equipment and Facilities

▶ Gym

▶ Kicking shields (optional)

▶ Folded panel mats (optional)

Warm-Ups

Begin with a cardiorespiratory warm-up and follow with a series of exercises that safely stretch all major muscle groups.

Procedure

1. Begin this lesson by drilling all of the leg techniques, including the knee, front, side, and back kicks. Students should execute kicks from a defensive stance and follow your cadence. If time permits, ask students to form small groups and practice kicking into a shield or folded panel mat.

2. Demonstrate the first release for a rear bear hug. This technique is fairly simple, but requires the victim to strike or grab the groin area. In an actual self-defense situation, if the assailant is male, the victim should grab the genitalia; if the assailant is female, the victim should strike the pubic bone. Caution the students to follow all safety procedures and emphasize that they should not actually make contact with their partners' groins. Students should practice delivering strikes *near* their partners' groins in slow motion.

3. Demonstrate the second release for a rear bear hug, which includes the technique of horse stance and backward elbow strike. Emphasize that students must move quickly away from the assailant after completing the release.

4. End the class by demonstrating the front bear hug release. This release utilizes the knee kick.

Conclusion

Review and discuss the lesson's targeted vital areas. Emphasize that the releases from this lesson will not work if the assailant has lifted the victim off the ground. Eventually, the assailant will have to put the victim down again, and this is when the technique can be effective. Ask students to discuss the use of their legs for a prerelease attack.

Day 15

Day	Skill	Release	Activity	
			Title	Handout
Day 15			• Deescalating a Potential Confrontation, page 95	• Deescalation Task Sheets, pages 96-98

Objectives

Students will be able to do the following:

1. Determine how their spoken and body languages can escalate situations.
2. Demonstrate how to deescalate several potential confrontations through role playing.
3. Cooperate with the group to complete a role-playing task sheet.
4. Demonstrate releases from single, double, and two-handed grabs; a full nelson hold and its variation; a head hold; and all variations on the front and rear bear hugs.

Equipment and Facilities

▶ Gym
▶ Chairs
▶ Handouts: Deescalation Task Sheets, pages 96-98
▶ Pencils

Warm-Ups

Begin with a cardiorespiratory warm-up and follow with a series of exercises that safely stretch all major muscle groups.

Procedure

1. Create a lecture-based discussion on the meaning and implications of escalating or deescalating potentially volatile situations (see Deescalating a Potential Confrontation, page 95).
2. Place students into groups of three. Provide task sheets for each student and explain the procedure for completing them. Students will take turns acting as assailant, victim, and recorder. Each scenario calls for all three roles, and each student should play each role during the course of the three scenarios.
3. Students should return the task sheets when finished. If groups finish early, they may practice previously learned skills, such as the wrist releases from single, double, and two-handed grabs, and releases from the full nelson holds, head hold, and variations on the front and rear bear hugs.

Conclusion

Go over the task sheets with the students and answer any questions they have about the lesson.

Day 16

Day	Skill	Release	Activity	
			Title	Handout
Day 16	*Review* • Elbow strikes, page 49	*Review* • Full nelson 1, page 64 • Full nelson 2, page 66 • Head hold, page 68		• Crime-Prevention Tips, page 79

Objectives

Students will be able to do the following:

1. Execute a release from a head hold with a partner.
2. Use their free hands and legs as weapons during release techniques.
3. Identify the contact points with a partner.
4. Cooperate with a partner, following all safety precautions.
5. Review and drill the releases for a full nelson with a partner.
6. Review and drill elbow strikes.
7. Identify fundamental crime-prevention tips for home and school.

Equipment and Facilities

▶ Gym
▶ Handout: Crime-Prevention Tips, page 79

Warm-Ups

Begin with a cardiorespiratory warm-up and follow with a series of exercises that safely stretch all major muscle groups.

Procedure

1. Start the lesson by reviewing upward, backward, and side elbow strikes. Remind students to hold their biceps close to their forearms. Drill students on technique and use of elbow strikes.
2. Review the head hold release. Demonstrate the technique's execution. Remind students that they must drop low to the ground in order for this release to work. Ask them to slowly practice the head hold and release with a partner. As they become comfortable with the technique, they can start to execute the release more quickly.
3. Discuss using free arms and legs as a potential weapon. Have students experiment with different techniques for a prerelease attack.
4. Review full nelson releases, prerelease attacks, and possible follow-up techniques, such as a back kick.

Conclusion

Discuss the lesson's contact points. Remind students to run away from an attacker whenever possible. The first line of defense in a potential conflict is avoidance. Review Crime-Prevention Tips and summarize key points.

Day 17

Day	Skill	Release	Activity	
			Title	Handout
Day 17		*Teach* • Front choke, page 70 • Rear choke, page 72		

Objectives

Students will be able to do the following:

1. Execute releases from the front and rear choke positions and move quickly away from the assailant.
2. Demonstrate comprehension of the severity of this attack.
3. Demonstrate using their free hands and legs as potential weapons during a prerelease attack.
4. Cooperate with a partner, adhering to all safety precautions.

Equipment and Facilities

Gym

Warm-Ups

Begin with a cardiorespiratory warm-up and follow with a series of exercises that safely stretch all major muscle groups.

Procedure

1. Demonstrate the full technique for the front choke hold and release.
2. Break down each part of the release, and drill the students individually. Make sure that every student performs the technique correctly. Emphasize the portion of the release where the victim places an armpit over the assailant's fingers.
3. Ask the students to choose a partner. Again, break the movement down into parts. Do not let the students do the whole movement at this point. Remind them to defend themselves by "scrunching" their necks. Make sure they understand how dangerous this type of attack is. In a real situation, a continued choke hold will result in loss of consciousness and eventual death.
4. When all the students can complete the movement, ask them to perform the whole technique in one fluid motion and run away from the assailant. Remind students that the assailant is trying to kill them and they must respond accordingly.
5. Discuss the use of the hands and legs as prerelease weapons. Have students experiment with a prerelease technique.
6. Follow the same procedure for the rear choke.

Conclusion

Remind students that they must move quickly but effectively while executing the front and back choke releases. Emphasize that they must exploit the assailant's fingers, the weakest part of the hold.

Days 18 and 19

Day	Skill	Release	Activity	
			Title	Handout
Days 18 and 19			• Self-Defense Scenarios, page 102	• Self-Defense Scenarios: Four-Week Unit (20 days), page 105

Objectives

Students will be able to do the following:

1. Analyze potentially dangerous situations and determine the best course of action.
2. Demonstrate self-defense moves that are practical and efficient for each scenario.
3. Evaluate the effectiveness of their chosen self-defense techniques.

Equipment and Facilities

▶ Gym
▶ Chairs
▶ Mats
▶ Handout: Self-Defense Scenarios (four-week unit), page 105

Warm-Ups

Begin with a cardiorespiratory warm-up and follow with a series of exercises that safely stretch all major muscle groups.

Procedure

1. Create a list of scenarios that will allow the students to use their skills either to protect themselves or to defuse a potentially dangerous situation. This lesson is a continuation of day 10, but includes more scenarios. It takes two days to complete and applies all of the previously learned self-defense skills and knowledge.
2. Ask students to form groups of four and to work on the activity sheet. The groups may either work independently to complete the entire activity sheet or complete each section separately. At the end of the class or after each scenario, bring the class together and analyze how the situation might have been either prevented or defused. Let students demonstrate their chosen release or technique for each scenario.

Conclusion

Remind students again that the key to self-defense is to use common sense, trust their instincts, and avoid conflict. Assailants must have three factors in order to commit a crime: desire, ability, and opportunity. Invite students to make comments or ask questions.

Note: You can also use these two days to assess individual physical skills. Place students in groups to perform individual physical skills with your cadence. Determine grades with the sample skill testing sheet from day 9 (see page 16) and the Individual Release Assessment Rubric from day 10 (see page 18).

Day 20

Day	Skill	Release	Activity	
			Title	**Handout**
Day 20			• Legal Aspects of Self-Defense, page 121	• You Be the Judge, page 123

Objectives

Students will be able to do the following:

1. Define the terms *felony* and *misdemeanor*.
2. Summarize the basic legal aspects of self-defense.
3. Cooperate with their groups to complete the jigsaw activity.

Equipment and Facilities

▶ Gym
▶ Informational posters (see Legal Aspects of Self-Defense, page 121)
▶ Tape
▶ Handout: You Be the Judge, page 123

Procedure

1. Create four posters with information on the legal aspects of self-defense (see Legal Aspects of Self-Defense, page 121), number them 1 to 4, and post them around the gym. Students will use the information on the posters to answer the questions on the handout.

2. Ask the students to form groups of four, and assign each member of the group a number from 1 to 4. Students are responsible for learning the information on the poster that corresponds to their assigned numbers, then sharing what they have learned with the group. In this way, the groups learn the information on all four posters.

3. Distribute the handout You Be the Judge to each group. Ask the students to answer the questions that follow each scenario using information from the posters. Students may return to the posters to review the material.

4. After students have completed the handout, bring the class together to discuss their responses to each scenario. Give them the correct answers and explain any legal issues that might be unclear.

Conclusion

Review any questions concerning the legal issues of self-defense.

► Part 2 ◄

Skills

Defensive Stance, Evasive Step, and Safety Yell

Focus

In this lesson, students will learn to project confidence in their posture and movements by being introduced to a defensive stance that is strong and balanced, and to an evasive step that allows for ease of movement. Students will also learn the safety yell, which is a shout at the moment of attack that adds both physical and mental force to the blow.

Objectives

Students will be able to do the following:

1. Demonstrate a defensive stance that is strong and balanced, and allows for ease of movement.
2. Demonstrate an evasive step for ease of movement.
3. Demonstrate a safety yell.
4. Identify when and why the safety yell should be used.

Equipment and Facilities

Gym

Protective Stance, Evasive Step, and Safety Yell

Organization	Extensions	Refinement cues
Step 1 • Teacher demonstration • Drill students individually.	Introduction to stance: Students demonstrate a defensive stance. Students take a partial sideways stance to their potential assailant. The stance has a wide, stable base, with one foot in front of the other and the knees bent (see figure 2.1a). The arms are held up in front to protect the body and face. The elbows remain in. Hands can remain open or closed (see figure 2.1b). Students keep their eyes straight ahead and maintain an assertive attitude.	• Wide base • Knees bent • Hands up • Eye contact
Step 2 Teacher demonstration	Introduction to evasive step: Students must maintain balance, and be alert and ready to move in any direction. The evasive step is a footwork maneuver that allows the student to assess the situation from a neutral distance. It also allows the student to be prepared for an escalation in the situation.	• Be in balance. • Maintain defensive arms.
Step 3 Drill students individually.	Moving to the left and right: To move to the right from a left-foot-forward stance, students move their back feet to the right and then take a step backward, ending in a right-foot-forward defensive stance (see figure 2.2a). To move to the left, students move their back feet to the left and then take a step backward, ending in a left-foot-forward defensive stance (see figure 2.2b).	• Move back foot across. • Move front foot back.
Step 4 Students practice with partners. Initially, students may choose their own partners for emotional safety.	Evasive side step with a partner: Partners face each other, holding their arms down. One student is designated the assailant, the other as the target. The assailant moves into the target's space. The target immediately takes an evasive step and a defensive stance. Repeat both sides.	• Centerline, eye contact, and stance • Hands up
Step 5 Teacher demonstration	Introduction to safety yell: The safety yell is a shout that concentrates all one's energy, physical and mental, upon a given object. The safety yell displays the unremitting determination to achieve a goal. The sound is typically low, loud, and long. A student can choose a word, such as "No," or just make a sound. The safety yell gives force to the blow.	• Low • Loud • Long
Step 6 Partner practice	The intended target should perform a safety yell when the assailant moves into his or her space. The intended target maintains a defensive stance.	• Defensive stance • Safety yell

Figure 2.1 *(a)* A wide, stable base and a *(b)* defensive stance.

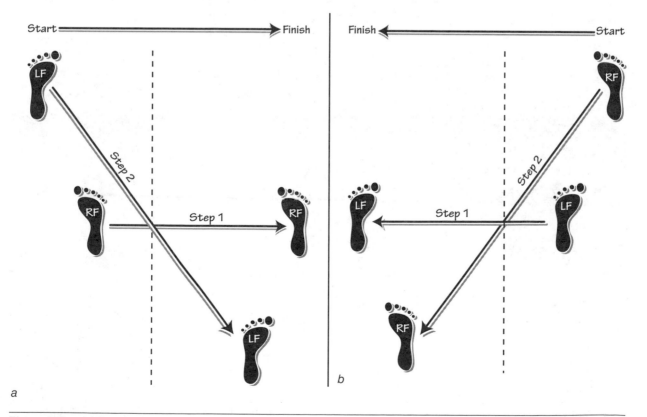

Figure 2.2 *(a)* Step to the right to end in a right-foot-forward stance and *(b)* step to the left to end in a left-foot-forward stance.

Horse Stance

Focus

The horse stance is a wide, low stance used in many martial art systems for punching drills, form patterns, and offensive and defensive techniques. Self-defense beginners use this stance to create a low, stable base for certain releases.

Objectives

Students will be able to move into a horse stance from a standing position to create a low, stable base.

Equipment and Facilities

Gym

Horse Stance

Organization	Extensions	Refinement cues
Step 1 Teacher demonstration	Introduction to horse stance: The horse stance is a wide, low stance. The stance should be approximately 30-36 inches (72-91 cm) wide, but the length will vary with height of each student. Knees are bent so that the thighs are at a 45-degree angle. Knees are held over the insteps, shin bones are perpendicular to the floor, and the back is kept straight.	• Thighs at 45-degree angle • Knees over instep • Back straight
Step 2 Drill students individually.	Students move sideways into horse stance from a standing position (see figure 2.3a). Students move backward into horse stance from a standing position, creating a sideways horse stance to the front (see figure 2.3b).	• Knees over instep • Back straight
Step 3 Drill students individually.	In a front horse stance, students perform front punches with alternating fists (see figure 2.3c). Both arms stop and start together. A safety yell can be executed on each forward punch or after a set number of punches. Teacher counts out each punch. Safety: This stance can cause pain to the thighs if students remain too long in the position.	• Stay down • Back straight • Arms stop and start together.

Figure 2.3 (a) Stepping sideways into a horse stance, (b) view from the side with the arms up, and (c) front punches from a horse stance.

Knee Kick

Focus

In this lesson, students will demonstrate a defensive stance and aim a knee kick toward an attacker's groin area. Students will identify and demonstrate the point of contact while working with a partner.

Objectives

Students will be able to do the following:

1. Demonstrate a defensive stance that is strong and balanced.
2. Demonstrate a successful knee kick, using proper form and power.
3. Execute a safety yell with the knee kick.
4. Identify the contact points for the kick.
5. Cooperate with a partner, adhering to all safety rules.

Equipment and Facilities

Gym

Knee Kick

Organization	Extensions	Refinement cues
Step 1 • Teacher demonstration • Drill students individually.	Introduction to knee kick technique and points of aim: The knee kick is intended to hit an attacker in the groin area. Students take a defensive stance. Students pretend that they have a stick between their hands (see figure 2.4a). Keeping their backs straight, students bring up the back knee and attempt to break the imaginary stick (see figure 2.4b). Students practice this movement, following teacher's cadence.	• Break the stick. • Knee high • Back straight
Step 2 Partner drill	Knee technique with partner: The assailant places his or her hands on the intended target's shoulders (see figure 2.4c). The target places his or her hands to the outside of the assailant's arms. As the target attempts the knee kick, he or she should pull the assailant toward the knee and perform a safety yell. Safety: Watch for students being too aggressive and hitting their heads when performing the technique. Avoid contact.	• Break the stick. • Back leg for knee technique • Safety yell
Step 3 Partner drill	Have student take a defensive stance. Assailant steps in to grab the target at the shoulders or neck. The target performs a knee kick with a safety yell. Repeat both sides.	• Eye contact • Defensive stance • Back leg for knee strike • Pull assailant in. • Safety yell

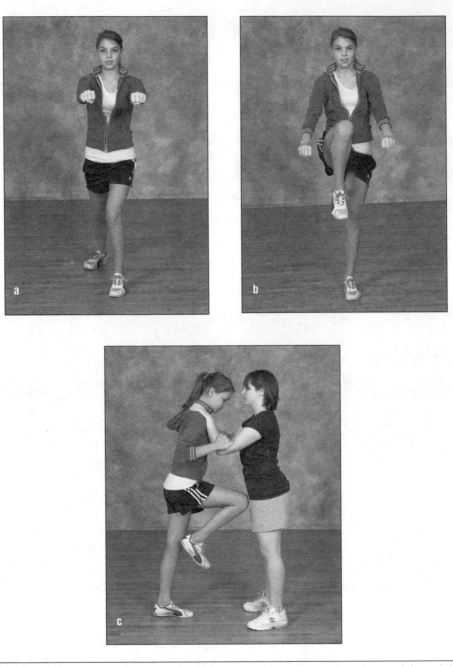

Figure 2.4 *(a)* Pretending to have a stick in hands, *(b)* breaking the imaginary stick, and *(c)* using this same motion against an assailant with their hands on a target's shoulders.

Front Kick

Focus

The front kick is executed from the defensive stance with either the leading or the back foot. Students will demonstrate using the toe of the shoe, the ball of the foot, or the heel to make contact with their target. Students will learn that in all physical encounters, their goal is to either blind or disable their assailant so that he or she can no longer see or walk.

Objectives

Students will be able to do the following:

1. Execute the front kick from a defensive stance.
2. Use the toe of the shoe, the ball of the foot, or the heel to perform a front kick.
3. Identify the contact points for this kick, including the groin and the knee.

Equipment and Facilities

▶ Gym
▶ Kicking bags or folded mats (optional)
▶ Paper (optional)

Front Kick

Organization	Extensions	Refinement cues
Step 1 • Teacher demonstration • Drill students individually.	Introduction of front kick: The front kick is executed from a defensive stance. It can be done by the leading or back foot. The student lifts the knee upward to the front of the body (see figure 2.5a). The foot is flexed. The foot is then extended toward the intended target (see figure 2.5b). Contact is made with the ball of the foot, tip of the shoe, or heel (see figure 2.5c). Points of aim should be the groin area or the knee.	• Defensive stance • Stay balanced. • Knee up • Flex foot. • Extend foot. • Return to flex. • Down
Step 2 Drill students individually.	Front kick drills: Students perform the front kick using ball of foot, tip of shoe, and heel. Teacher counts out each step of the kick and students perform kick. Students perform whole kick on one count.	• Knee up • Flex. • Extend. • Flex. • Down
Step 3 Partner drill	Front kick with partner: Students face partners at a safe distance. One student stands with hands in front of the groin. Other student aims the front kick toward the partner's groin (see figure 2.5d). Have students take turns kicking by the count. Do not let students kick unless directed to do so. Students use ball of foot, tip of shoe, and heel. Safety: Have each student keep a safe distance and follow teacher's count.	• Knee up • Flex. • Extend. • Flex. • Down
Step 4 Partner drill	Front kick with grab: One partner grabs the other's wrist (see figure 2.5e). Intended target takes a defensive stance and performs a front kick with ball of foot, tip of shoe, and heel of foot. Point of aim is groin and kneecap. As students perform kick, they may use a safety yell. Safety: Students must not make any contact with partners when practicing kicks.	• Kick. • Aim. • Safety yell

Variations

▶ Kicking Bags—Students aim kicks at a bag being held by a partner. Students should kick slowly and gently at first, then gradually build intensity as they gain skill and confidence.

▶ Folded Mats—Students may direct their kicks into folded mats that are propped up vertically against a wall or held by several students.

▶ Paper—Students may practice kicking an 8.5-by-11-inch (22 by 28 cm) sheet of paper that is held by another student. The partners holding the sheets of paper must hold the paper out to the side, away from their bodies, with their fingers curled tightly. Warn students to avoid their partners' hands and arms when kicking.

Figure 2.5 *(a)* Lifting the knee to the front of the body, *(b)* extending the foot toward a target, *(c)* making contact with the ball of the foot, tip of the shoe, or heel, *(d)* a kick to the groin, and *(e)* front kick with grab by assailant.

Side Kick

Focus

This technique is executed in the same manner as the front kick, but angles the kick to the side and uses the knife edge of the foot. Teach students to aim the kick at the side edge of the assailant's knee to limit the assailant's movement.

Objectives

Students will be able to do the following:

1. Execute a side kick from a balanced and stable defensive stance.
2. Identify the points of aim for the side kick.
3. Cooperate with a partner, adhering to all safety rules.

Equipment and Facilities

▶ Gym
▶ Kicking bags (optional)
▶ Folded mats (optional)

Side Kick

Organization	Extensions	Refinement cues
Step 1 • Teacher demonstration • Drill students individually.	Introduction to side kick: The side kick is executed in the same manner as the front kick, but angles the kick to the side. The kick is typically done on the leading foot. Students should aim the kick at the side edge of the attacker's knee using the knife edge of the foot. Students lift the knee upward in front of the body. The foot is flexed. The knife edge of the foot is extended toward the target (see figure 2.6a). In all techniques, the victim's goal is to either blind or disable the attacker so he or she can no longer see or walk. Students perform the side kick using the knife edge of foot. Teacher counts out each step of the kick and students perform kick. Students perform whole kick on one count.	• Knee up • Flex foot. • Extend knife edge. • Flex foot. • Down
Step 2 Partner drill	Side kick with partner: Students perform a cross grab with a partner and aim a side kick to the knee (see figure 2.6b). Safety: No contact allowed. All kicks are directed at an area past the partner's body.	• Knee up • Flex. • Extend knife edge. • Flex. • Stay balanced. • Down

Variations

▶ Kicking Bags—Students aim kicks at a bag being held by a partner. Students should kick slowly and gently at first, then gradually build intensity as they gain skill and confidence.
▶ Folded Mats—Students may direct their kicks into folded mats that are propped up vertically against a wall or held by several students.

Figure 2.6 *(a)* Foot extended toward a target and *(b)* a cross grab and side kick to knee.

Back Kick and Variation

Focus

Students will demonstrate the back kick from both standing and kneeling positions. They will later combine this technique with the full nelson release.

Objectives

Students will be able to do the following:

1. Properly execute a back kick while standing.
2. Properly execute a back kick while kneeling.
3. Identify contact points for the back kick.

Equipment and Facilities

- ▶ Gym
- ▶ Folded mats
- ▶ Kicking pads (optional)

Back Kick

Organization	Extensions	Refinement cues
Step 1 Teacher demonstration	Introduction to the back kick: The back kick is a powerful kick that requires good balance and technique. The student brings the knee up with the foot flexed, then looks over corresponding shoulder and extends heel backward. The extended leg must rub against the supporting leg. Students should be cautioned not to hook or swing the leg around. It is a backward kick, sometimes called a *mule kick*. Depending on the position of the attacker, the heel can be directed to the kneecap or to the groin.	• Stance • Knee up • Foot flexed • Look over shoulder. • Heel kicks backward. • Rub the supporting leg. • Return to position.
Step 2 Drill students individually.	Students place their hands on a wall for balance (see figure 2.7a). Bring knee up with flexed foot. Look over corresponding shoulder. Extend leg backward, make contact with heel, and return knee to forward position (see figure 2.7b).	• Knee up • Flexed foot • Look. • Heel • Rub supporting leg.
Step 3 Drill students individually.	Students complete whole kick without wall support.	• Stance • Knee up • Flex. • Look. • Extend heel.
Step 4 Partner drill	With partner, student performs back kick into a folded mat or kicking bag.	• Stance • Knee up • Flex. • Look. • Extend heel.
Step 5 Teacher demonstration	Teacher demonstrates the back kick from a kneeling position. The student brings the knee to the stomach, looks over the corresponding shoulder, and kicks backwards with the heel (see figure 2.7c). Depending on the position of the attacker, the heel can be directed to the kneecap or to the groin.	• Knee to stomach • Look. • Kick with heel.

(continued)

Back Kick *(continued)*

Organization	Extensions	Refinement cues
Step 6 Drill students individually.	Students kneel on floor, bring knee in toward stomach, and look over corresponding shoulder, before extending heel backwards.	• Knee up • Look. • Extend heel. • Return to starting position.
Step 7 Partner drill	Student performs back kick from a kneeling position into a folded mat or kicking bag (see figure 2.7*d*).	• Knee up • Look. • Extend heel. • Return to starting position.

Figure 2.7   *(a)* Using the wall to get balance, *(b)* extending the leg backward, *(c)* a back kick from a kneeling position and *(d)* kicking a mat held by a partner.

Front and Reverse Punches

Focus

The arm movements in the front punch are used in the majority of hand techniques. The punch, however, is not the best technique to use in self-defense. The full extended arm at contact can easily collapse without adequate training, but the arm movement is generic to all other hand techniques. Students will learn how to form a fist, to chamber, and to execute a punch. The front punch is performed by using the arm on the same side as the front or leading leg. The reverse punch is executed by using the arm on the same side as the back leg.

Objectives

Students will be able to do the following:

1. Form a proper fist while performing front and reverse punches.
2. Perform the motions of the front and reverse punches correctly.
3. Identify the key aiming points on the body for these punches.

Equipment and Facilities

▶ Gym
▶ 8.5-by-11-inch (22 by 28 cm) sheets of paper (optional)

Front and Reverse Punches

Organization	Extensions	Refinement cues
Step 1 Teacher demonstration	Introduction to front punch: The front punch is not the best hand technique to use in a dangerous situation, but the arm movement is generic to all other hand techniques. Reverse punch is performed from a defensive stance. The arm corresponding to the rear leg is used. The front punch is performed by using the arm on the same side as the front or leading leg.	
Step 2 Teacher demonstration	The fist position: to make a secure fist, roll the fingers to the center of the palm and secure the thumb on the outside of the fist (see figure 2.8a). Safety: Contact with a loose fist can cause injury. Emphasize a strong fist.	
Step 3 Teacher demonstration	Chambering: The arm is brought back into position with the palm of hand facing upward. The forearm is level to the floor (see figure 2.8b). This arm position is called the "chamber." During the forward punch, the forearm rubs the side of the body. The arm begins to turn after the elbow clears the ribs or during the last 6 inches (15 cm) of the punch (see figure 2.8c).	• Chamber. • Turn.
Step 4 Teacher demonstration	Contact is made with the first knuckles. Keep wrist straight and firm.	Wrist firm
Step 5 Drill students individually.	Students perform the front or reverse punch from a defensive stance.	• Wrist firm • Rub side of body with arm. • Turn over the last 6 inches (15 cm).

Variations

▶ Paper—Students may practice aiming both front and reverse punches at an 8.5-by-11-inch (22 by 28 cm) sheet of paper that is held by another student (see figure 2.8d). The partners holding the sheets of paper must hold the paper out to the side, away from their bodies, with their fingers curled tightly.

▶ High, Low, and Middle Drills—Students should assume a defensive stance and practice punching at high, middle, and low body levels in time with your cadence.

▶ Horse Stance Punching Drill—Students should assume the horse stance and alternate punches in time with your cadence.

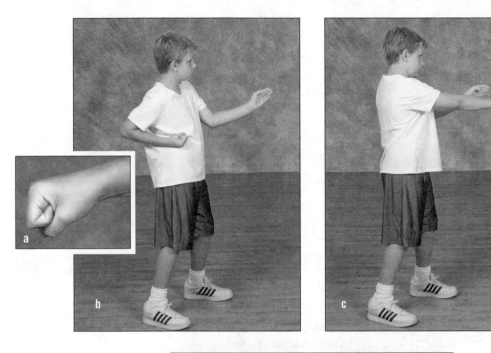

Figure 2.8 *(a)* A fist, *(b)* the forearm needs to be level to the floor, *(c)* punching forward, and *(d)* punching paper held by a partner.

Heel-of-Palm Strike

Focus

In this lesson, students will learn to execute the heel-of-palm strike and to make contact with the appropriate contact points on the assailant's body. They should aim this strike at the nose or the area under the chin. The technique can be done with the arm on the same side as the back foot or the front foot.

Objectives

Students will be able to do the following:

1. Execute a heel-of-palm strike from a defensive stance.
2. Identify the contact points for the strike.
3. Cooperate with a partner, adhering to all safety rules.

Equipment and Facilities

Gym

Heel-of-Palm Strike

Organization	Extensions	Refinement cues
Step 1 Teacher demonstration	Introduction to heel-of-palm strike: The heel of the palm is aimed at the nose or chin. The technique can be done with the arm on the same side as the back or leading leg. The technique will be stronger if it is executed off the back leg. Take a defensive stance, bring one arm back into the chamber position (hand opened or closed). The palm should face upward in either position. As the palm of the hand extends forward, the arm turns to add strength to the technique (see figure 2.9a).	• Defensive stance • Palm up and in chamber • Turn. • Aim with heel of palm.
Step 2 Drill students individually.	Students drill technique following the cadence of the instructor.	• Chamber. • Turn. • Aim with heel of palm. • Return to defensive stance.
Step 3 Partner drill	Ask students to grab either wrist of a partner and perform a heel-of-palm strike, aiming to the nose or under the chin (see figure 2.8b). Variation: Have student grab sleeve or upper arm of a partner.	• Chamber. • Turn. • Aim with heel of palm. • Return to defensive stance.

Figure 2.9 *(a)* Extending the palm forward from a defensive stance and *(b)* a heel-of-palm strike aimed at the nose or chin of an assailant.

Back Fist Strike

Focus

In this lesson, students will demonstrate the correct back fist technique from a defensive stance. In the back fist strike, students aim a blow at the assailant's nose with the intent to impair his or her sight so they will have an opportunity to escape.

Objectives

Students will be able to do the following:

1. Execute a proper back fist strike from a defensive stance.
2. Identify the key contact points for the back fist strike.
3. Cooperate with partner during the paper drill.

Equipment and Facilities

▶ Gym

▶ 8.5-by-11-inch (22 by 28 cm) sheets of paper (optional)

Back Fist Strike

Organization	Extensions	Refinement cues
Step 1 Teacher demonstration	Introduction to back fist strike: The back fist strike is a technique that is aimed at the nose. The back fist strike is executed by snapping the forearm forward with a firm wrist. The motion is similar to snapping a towel. The knuckle edge of the back of the hand makes contact with the nose. Hitting the nose with force will cause the eyes to tear up. The result is that the assailant will not have clear vision.	• Knuckle edge • Snap a towel.
Step 2 Drill students individually.	Students take a defensive stance with legs to the side and balanced, one foot in front of the other, and the knees bent. Arms are up in front with elbows held in. The arm aligned with the front foot is clenched into a fist (see figure 2.10a). The arm corresponding to the front foot is typically used. The back fist strike is executed by snapping the forearm forward with a firm wrist. The motion is similar to snapping a towel. The knuckle edge of the back of the hand makes contact with the nose (see figure 2.10b).	• Defensive stance • Balanced • Tight fist • Elbows in • Firm wrist • Snap a towel.
Step 3 Partner drill	One student holds paper to the side with fingers curled tight. The partner snaps the fist forward and back, aiming at the paper. Safety: If the elbow begins to hurt, the student is bending the wrist. Remind students to have a firm wrist.	• Wrist firm and secure • Fast • Snap back. • Contact back of hand, first two knuckles

Variations

▶ Back Fist Strike and Reverse Punch Drill—Ask students to combine the back fist strike with a reverse punch (see page 43). Drill students individually.

▶ Paper—Ask students to repeat the preceding drill with a partner holding a piece of paper. They should aim a back fist strike into the paper, followed by a reverse punch. They may substitute a heel-of-palm strike for the reverse punch.

Figure 2.10 *(a)* Clenched fist in a defensive stance and *(b)* how the back of the hand contacts with the nose of an assailant.

Elbow Strikes

Focus

The elbow strike can be delivered in a variety of ways. The elbow can be swung upward, backward, to the sides, or around in a circular motion. Students will learn to execute the front, back, and side elbow strikes, and to aim at the appropriate contact points on an assailant's body.

Objectives

Students will be able to do the following:

1. Execute front, side, and back elbow strikes from a defensive stance.
2. Identify the points of aim for the front, side, and back elbow strikes.
3. Cooperate with a partner during situational drills, adhering to all safety rules.

Equipment and Facilities

Gym

Elbow Strikes

Organization	Extensions	Refinement cues
Step 1 Teacher demonstration	Introduction to the upward elbow: The upward elbow begins in the chamber position and the hand in the fist position. The arm stays tight to the body as the elbow moves upward (see figure 2.11a). The palm of the first hand stops at the ear with palm facing the ear.	• Chamber. • Tight fist • Bicep sticks to forearm.
Step 2 Drill students individually.	Students drill the upward elbow movement following the teacher's cadence The upward elbow is aimed at the nose or under the chin.	• Tight fist • Bicep sticks to forearm. • Palm faces ear.
Step 3 Teacher demonstration	Introduction to the backward elbow: The technique starts in a defensive stance with arms held in front of the body. Make a fist with the arm on the side of the back leg and forcibly bring it back into the chamber position. This creates the backward elbow. Look over the corresponding shoulder for a visual (see figure 2.11b).	• Tight fist • Look over shoulder.
Step 4 Drill students individually.	Students drill the backward elbow movement following the teacher's cadence. The backward elbow can be aimed at an attacker's nose or solar plexus when grabbed from behind.	• Tight fist • Bicep sticks to forearm.
Step 5 Teacher demonstration	Introduction to the side elbow: The technique starts in a defensive stance with arms in front of the body. The side elbow should be executed off the front leg. Make a fist and drop the arm in front of the body, level to the floor, then move the elbow sideways. The fist should not travel beyond the midline of the body (see figure 2.11c).	• Tight fist • Drop level in front. • Stop at midline.
Step 6 Drill students individually.	Students drill side elbow movement following the teacher's cadence. The side elbow is aimed at the partner's head, preferably at the nose or the temple.	• Stop at midline. • Off of front foot

(continued)

Organization	Extensions	Refinement cues
Step 7 Partner drill	Each student follows the teacher's commands and slowly executes the proper elbow technique and points of aim.	• Upward elbow: chin and nose • Backward elbow: solar plexus • Side elbow: nose or temple
Step 8 Partner drill	Ask students to face each other and have one partner grab the other's wrist (right to left). Intended target assumes a defensive stance and performs an upward elbow strike to the assailant's chin and nose. Students move very slowly and without any contact. Variation: Have students grab a partner's sleeve or upper arm. Safety: No contact during strikes. All movements are performed deliberately and slowly.	• Defensive stance • Move into technique for distance. • Bicep sticks to forearm.
Step 9 Partner drill	Ask students to grab a partner's wrist (right to left). Intended target turns right shoulder toward assailant and performs a right side elbow to the chin (see figure 2.11*d*). Variation: Have students grab a partner's sleeve or upper arm. Safety: No contact during strikes. All movements are performed deliberately and slowly.	• Defensive stance • Stop at midline.
Step 10 Partner drill	Ask students to place their hands on a partner's shoulders from behind. Partner performs a backward elbow strike into the assailant's solar plexus (see figure 2.11*e*). Safety: No contact during strikes. All movements are performed deliberately and slowly.	• Defensive stance • Look over corresponding shoulder. • Elbow off back leg for distance

(continued)

Figure 2.11 *(a)* The elbow moving upward, *(b)* looking backward and extending the elbow, *(c)* moving the elbow sideways, . . .

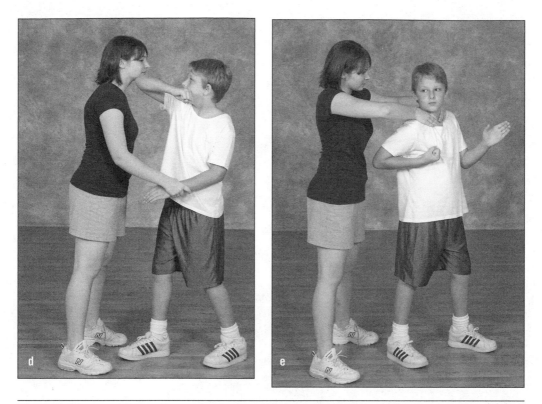

Figure 2.11   . . . (d) the elbow going to an assailant's chin with a partner grab, and (e) an elbow going to the solar plexus of an assailant.

▷ Part 3 ◁
Releases

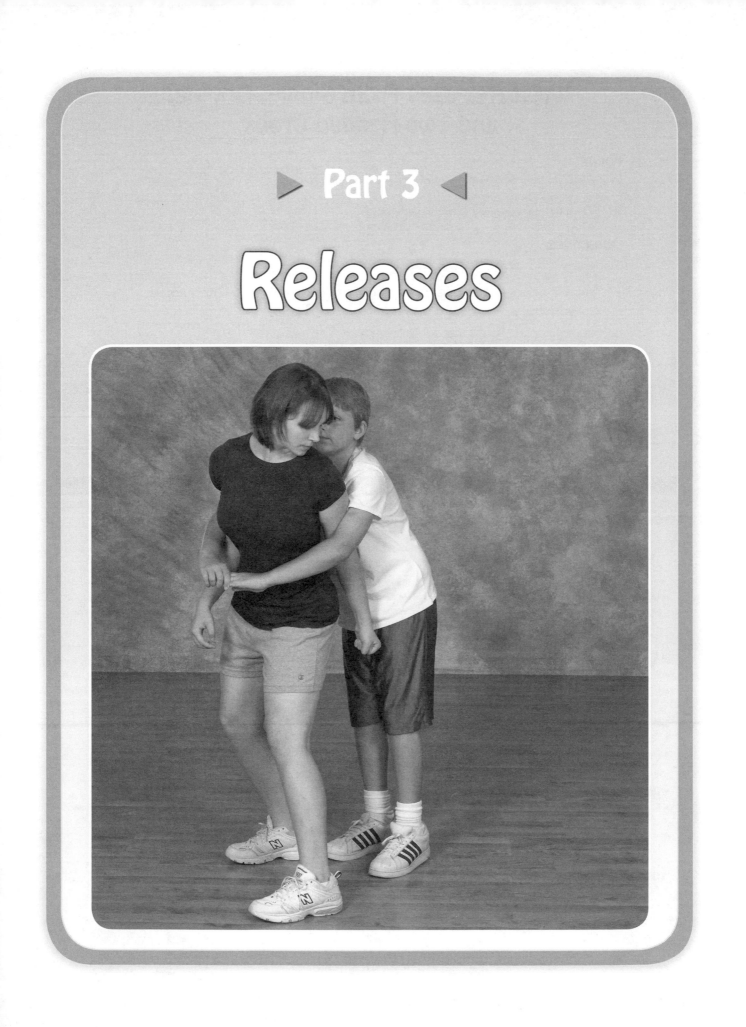

Wrist Releases From Single, Double, and Two-Handed Grabs

Focus

In this lesson, students will be introduced to their first release techniques. They will learn how to escape from a single, a double, and a two-handed wrist grab, and to combine hand and foot techniques with the wrist releases.

Objectives

Students will be able to do the following:

1. Demonstrate a wrist release from a single, a double, and a two-handed grab.
2. Combine the wrist release with foot and hand techniques.
3. Identify contact points that will help them execute a wrist release.
4. Execute a safety yell at the moment of release.
5. Cooperate with a partner, adhering to all safety rules.

Equipment and Facilities

Gym

Releases From Single and Double Wrist Holds

Organization	Extensions	Refinement cues
Step 1 Teacher demonstration	Introduction of wrist releases: This technique is appropriate if a target's wrist is grabbed by an assailant. The natural reaction is to pull away from the assailant, but this movement will only tighten the grip. Instead, the target should roll the arm toward the assailant's thumb, which is the weakest point of the grab, and then pull the arm away, maintaining a defensive stance.	• Defensive stance • Balanced • Roll downward toward assailant's thumb.
Step 2 • Teacher demonstration • Partner drill	Assailant grabs target's wrist diagonally (right hand to right wrist). Target assumes a balanced, defensive stance and gets ready to run at the release. Target rolls the arm toward the assailant's thumb. For example, if the target's right wrist is grabbed, he or she should roll the arm to the right, down, and away (see figure 3.1a).	• Balanced • Roll outward and down toward assailant's thumb.
Step 3 • Teacher demonstration • Partner drill	Assailant grabs target's wrist straight ahead (left hand to right wrist). The target assumes a balanced, defensive stance and gets ready to run at the release. The target rolls the arm downward toward the assailant's thumb. For example, if the target's right wrist is grabbed, he or she should roll the arm to the left (see figure 3.1b).	• Balanced • Roll inward and down toward assailant's thumb.
Step 4 • Teacher demonstration • Partner drill	If both wrists are grabbed, the intended target turns both arms in toward the center. Again, the arm movement is directed toward the assailant's thumbs (see figure 3.1c). The target is prepared to quickly move away from the assailant.	• Balanced • Roll inward and down. • Be prepared to run.
Step 5 • Teacher demonstration • Partner drill	If the assailant grabs one of the target's wrists with two hands, the target makes a fist with the grabbed arm (see figure 3.2a). The target then grabs the fist with his or her free arm and pulls it up and to the side toward the chest (see figure 3.2b). As the target moves the arm sideways, he or she is prepared to move quickly away from the assailant (see figure 3.2c).	• Balanced • Make a fist. • Pull upward and sideways to chest. • Be prepared to run.
Step 6 Partner drill	Partners practice the diagonal grab and straight ahead grab with the intended target moving away from the assailant after each release. The target should be very careful throughout this technique to maintain balance and a stance that will allow for a quick escape. The target can perform a safety yell at the moment of release.	• Balanced • Roll toward assailant's thumb. • Strong, quick motion • Safety yell • Run.

Organization	Extensions	Refinement cues
Step 7 Partner drill	Partners practice the double grab with the intended target moving away from the assailant and performing a safety yell at the release. Students should concentrate on balance.	• Balanced • Roll inward. • Strong, quick motion • Run.
Step 8 Partner drill	Partners practice the two-handed grab with the intended target moving away from the assailant at the release. Students should be careful not to bring arms upward into the face, but sideways toward the chest for safety.	• Balanced • Make a fist. • Pull upward and then sideways. • Run.

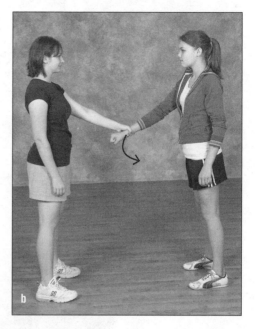

Figure 3.1 *(a)* A diagonal grab, *(b)* a straight ahead grab, and *(c)* a double grab.

Figure 3.2 *(a)* One wrist grabbed by two hands by the assailant, *(b)* target grabbing her own fist, and *(c)* pulling through the assailant's hands.

Variations

Release Drill From Single Wrist Holds

Students can now apply combinations of skills to an attack. Those acting as intended targets can execute a prerelease attack before attempting to escape from a hold. The elbow, heel-of-palm, or back fist strikes can be combined with the single wrist technique. Students should demonstrate a hand technique before the release, perform the release, and then escape.

Release Drill From Double Grab and Two-Handed Grab

Students can now apply a combination of skills to the double grab and the two-handed grab. Those acting as intended targets can execute a prerelease attack before attempting to escape from a hold. The front toe, heel, or ball-of-foot kicks can be combined with the double wrist release or two-handed grab. Students should execute a front kick before attempting the release. Students should take a defensive stance, perform a front kick off the rear leg, regain balance, perform the release, and then escape.

A combination of skills is advised when the assailant's grip is obviously too strong. The impact of the hand or leg technique will cause the assailant to loosen the grip on the wrist, allowing the victim a moment to escape.

Rear Bear Hug Release 1

Focus

There are several release variations for the rear bear hug. This release is one of the simplest to learn. The assailant grabs the victim from behind and pins his or her arms to the sides. Students will learn that by moving their hips slightly to the side they can perform a striking technique to the groin area.

Objectives

Students will be able to do the following:

1. Demonstrate a release from a rear bear hug.
2. Identify the contact points needed to assist in the rear bear hug release.
3. Cooperate with a partner, adhering to all safety precautions.

Equipment and Facilities

Gym

Rear Bear Hug Release 1

Organization	Extensions	Refinement cues
Step 1 Teacher demonstration	Introduction to the rear bear hug release: There are several variations to the rear bear hug. In this situation, the intended target is grabbed from behind and his or her arms are pinned to the sides. The target shifts his or her hips to the side and either directs a strike backward into the assailant's groin area or grabs his testicles and twists them.	• Shift hips. • Deliver a strike. • Grab and twist.
Step 2 Partner drill	With partners, adhering to all safety precautions, students practice being held in a bear hug and directing a strike near the groin (see figure 3.3a). Safety: Students should not make contact with the groin area, but just demonstrate the movement slowly.	• Shift hips. • Deliver a strike or grab and twist.
Step 3 Partner drill	With a partner, the intended target performs a prerelease attack by stomping on the assailant's instep (see figure 3.3, b-c). The stomp will both distract and hurt the assailant. The intended target then shifts the hips, strikes or grabs the assailant's groin, and moves quickly away from the assailant.	• Stomp. • Shift hips. • Deliver a strike or grab and twist. • Move quickly away.

Variation

Depending on the height of the assailant and the intended target, an alternate prerelease strike can be executed. The target can bend the head forward, and then aggressively thrust it backward into the assailant's nose. This technique will only work if both people are of comparable heights. The intended target then shifts the hips, strikes or grabs the assailant's groin area, and moves quickly away.

Safety

The head butt technique must be practiced slowly and with control. Do not let any student perform this technique quickly and forcefully.

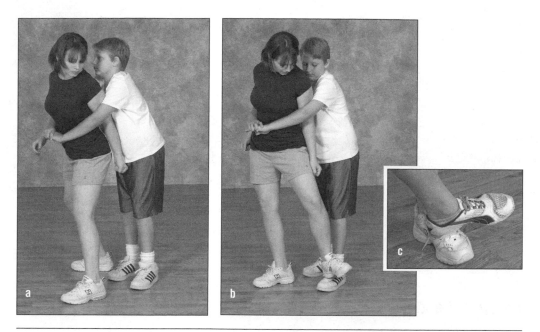

Figure 3.3 *(a)* Directing a strike near the groin of an assailant, *(b)* stomping on the assailant's instep, and *(c)* a closer look at the target's stomp on the assailant's instep.

Rear Bear Hug Release 2

Focus

Students will learn a second variation of the rear bear hug release. This release requires the use of the horse stance and the back elbow strike. After performing the release, students will be able to move forward and away from the attacker.

Objectives

Students will be able to do the following:

1. Execute a rear bear hug release with a horse stance and a back elbow strike.
2. Identify the contact points needed to assist in the rear bear hug release.
3. Execute a safety yell at the moment of the back elbow strike.
4. Cooperate with a partner, adhering to all safety precautions.

Equipment and Facilities

Gym

Rear Bear Hug Release 2

Organization	Extensions	Refinement cues
Step 1 Teacher demonstration	Introduction to rear bear hug release: This variation of the rear bear hug release requires the horse stance and a back elbow strike. The intended target is grabbed from behind with his or her arms pinned to the sides. The intended target drops into the horse stance and simultaneously shoots the arms downward, rolling them so that the back of the hands are facing together. The target lifts up assailant's arms slightly, looks over shoulder of the dominant elbow, and performs a back elbow strike to the attacker's solar plexus. The target then moves quickly forward and out of the assailant's grasp.	• Horse stance • Roll arms inward. • Back of hands face together. • Lift. • Elbow back
Step 2 Drill students individually.	Student faces forward, drops into horse stance, and shoots arms downward with back of the hands facing together (see figure 3.4a).	• Shoot arms down. • Back of the hands together
Step 3 Drill students individually.	Student completes horse stance and downward arm thrust, lifts arms slightly (see figure 3.4b), looks over shoulder of dominant elbow, and performs the back elbow strike (see figure 3.4c).	• Horse stance • Shoot arms down. • Lift. • Elbow strike
Step 4 Drill students individually.	Student completes rear bear hug release and elbow strike and moves quickly forward out of assailant's grasp.	• Lift. • Elbow strike • Move forward.
Step 5 Partner drill	Students perform whole technique with a partner (see figure 3.5, a-c). The elbow strike is directed toward the solar plexus or groin area and is accompanied by a safety yell. After delivering the elbow strike, the intended target moves quickly out of the assailant's grasp.	• Arms down • Lift. • Look. • Strike. • Safety yell • Run.

Figure 3.4 *(a)* Dropping into a horse stance with arms down, *(b)* horse stance with arms slightly up, and *(c)* looking over the shoulder for a strike.

Figure 3.5 A partner drill showing *(a)* dropping into a horse stance with arms down, *(b)* lifting the arms slightly, and *(c)* elbow strikes to solar plexus or groin.

Front Bear Hug Release

Focus

Students will be able to execute a release from a front bear hug in which their arms are pinned and they are facing the assailant. This release utilizes the knee kick.

Objectives

Students will be able to do the following:

1. Properly execute the release technique for a front bear hug.
2. Identify the contact points needed to assist in the release.
3. Execute a safety yell at the time of the knee kick.
4. Cooperate with a partner, adhering to all safety procedures.

Equipment and Facilities

Gym

Front Bear Hug

Organization	Extensions	Refinement cues
Step 1 Teacher demonstration	Introduction to release from front bear hug: In this technique, the assailant faces the intended target and grips his or her body, pinning the arms down. The target quickly assumes a stance with one foot in front of the other, pushes on the assailant's thighs to create space, and executes a knee kick to the groin. Safety: Students must move very slowly and must not make contact during kicks.	• Stance • Palms on hip joint • Push. • Knee kick
Step 2 Partner drill	As the assailant pins the target's arms down, the target places his or her feet so that one foot is in front of the other. The target's strongest leg should be to the back.	Stance
Step 3 Partner drill	The target places the palms of the hands on the assailant's hip joints and pushes forward (see figure 3.6a). The assailant's hips will move backward, creating space.	• Palms on hip joint • Push.
Step 4 Partner drill	The intended target then executes a knee kick to the assailant's groin area and breaks free from the grasp (see figure 3.6b).	• Knee kick • Break from assailant's grasp.
Step 5 Partner drill	Students should complete the technique in one smooth motion, executing a safety yell with the knee kick. Safety: Students must be in control of the knee movement and must not make contact during the knee kick.	• Stance • Push. • Knee and safety yell • Break away.

Figure 3.6 *(a)* Target pushing the assailant's hips away and *(b)* a knee kick to an assailant's groin.

Full Nelson Release 1

Focus

Students will learn a simple release for the full nelson hold. The full nelson refers to a wrestling hold in which an opponent stands behind the victim, thrusts his or her arms under the victim's armpits, and clasps his or her hands behind the victim's head. This release will be combined with the kneeling back kick.

Objectives

Students will be able to do the following:

1. Properly execute a simple release for the full nelson.
2. Identify the key elements needed for the full nelson release.
3. Identify hand and foot techniques that assist in the release technique.
4. Execute a safety yell during the back kick.
5. Work cooperatively with a partner, adhering to all safety rules.

Facilities and Equipment

▶ Gym
▶ Mats (optional)

Full Nelson Release 1

Organization	Extensions	Refinement cues
Step 1 Teacher demonstration	Introduction to full nelson release: This release requires speed, looseness, and agility. The target is grabbed from behind in a full nelson. The target lifts his or her arms straight up, then immediately drops straight down, and slips out of the grab. Safety: Students must commit to the drop, but they risk banging their knees on the floor. It is recommended that students perform this release on mats and tuck in their shirts.	• Straighten arms. • Drop loose and quick.
Step 2 Partner drill	Assailant grabs target from behind by thrusting his or her arms under the target's armpits and clasping hands behind the target's head (see figure 3.7a). The target lifts his or her arms straight up, then immediately drops down to the ground on the knees (see figure 3.7, b-c). The target must stay loose and agile. Safety: This release should be done on mats.	• Straighten arms. • Drop loose and quick. • Fall to knees.
Step 3 Partner drill	Full nelson release with back kick: Assailant grabs intended target in a full nelson. The target executes the downward drop and lands on the knees. The target looks over his or her shoulder and performs a backward kick aimed at the assailant's knee or groin (see figure 3.7d). Intended target performs a safety yell during the back kick. Safety: Students should be aware of the distance between partners and must not make contact during the kick.	• Straighten arms. • Drop loose and quick. • Fall to knees. • Look. • Kick with heel.

Figure 3.7 *(a)* A target in a full nelson hold, *(b)* target moves her arms overhead, *(c)* target dropping to her knees, and *(d)* target delivering a backward kick.

Full Nelson Release 2

Focus

Students will demonstrate a full nelson release that requires upper body strength. This release will not be suitable for all students, but it is another option for a release from a full nelson hold. Students will be asked to combine several skills, including the horse stance, evasive step, heel-of-palm strike, and full punch.

Objectives

Students will be able to do the following:

1. Properly execute a release from the full nelson.
2. Demonstrate a proper horse stance.
3. Demonstrate an evasive step and deliver a heel-of-palm strike and full punch.
4. Execute a safety yell at the moment of release and hand strike.
5. Identify the contact points needed to assist in the full nelson release.
6. Cooperate with a partner, adhering to all safety rules.

Equipment and Facilities

Gym

Full Nelson Release 2

Organization	Extensions	Refinement cues
Step 1 Teacher demonstration	Introduction to full nelson release: This release is for students with strong upper bodies. As the target is grabbed in the full nelson, he or she will move or tilt to the side to throw off the assailant's balance. The target brings the arms upward and presses them backward and downward to release the assailant's grip around the neck. The target assumes the horse stance.	• Tilt. • Press back. • Break downward. • Horse stance
Step 2 Partner drill	Assailant grabs target in a full nelson. The intended target lifts the arms straight up, presses back, and tilts to one side (see figure 3.8a).	• Arms up • Press back. • Tilt.
Step 3 Partner drill	The target brings the arms downward as he or she moves opposite to the tilt into a horse stance (see figure 3.8b). Note: The target must press the arms backward toward the assailant's body as he or she begins the downward motion.	• Arms up • Press back. • Tilt. • Break downward. • Horse stance
Step 4 Partner drill	The intended target completes full release, uses a safety yell, and then performs an evasive step. The target then faces assailant in a defensive stance and delivers a heel-of-palm strike to the assailant's chin or nose (see figure 3.8c).	• Arms up • Press back. • Tilt. • Break downward. • Horse stance • Evasive step • Heel-of-palm to chin or nose

Figure 3.8 *(a)* A target in a full nelson hold with her arms overhead, *(b)* target moves arms down and into a horse stance, and *(c)* target performs heel-of-palm strike to her assailant's nose or chin.

Variation

Students can perform a multitude of techniques as they take the defensive stance after the release, including the front kick, back fist strike, and front punch.

If the target moves forward after the release and does not turn to face the assailant, he or she can perform a back kick.

Head Hold Release

Focus

Students will be able to execute a release when their heads are grasped by one of an attacker's arms. Emphasize the importance of using the free hands and legs for a pre-release attack.

Objectives

Students will be able to do the following:

1. Execute a proper release from a head hold.
2. Demonstrate the use of their free hands and legs in a prerelease attack.
3. Identify the contact points needed to assist in a head hold release.
4. Execute a safety yell at the moment of the leg or hand strike.
5. Cooperate with a partner, adhering to all safety rules.

Equipment and Facilities

Gym

Head Hold Release

Organization	Extensions	Refinement cues
Step 1 Teacher demonstration	Introduction to head hold release: The assailant will use one arm to grasp the intended target's head around the neck from behind. The assailant's forearm will be pressed against the target's neck. The target must be aware that this is a partial strangling attack. He or she must immediately protect the throat by creating a leverage maneuver to push up the assailant's elbow and pull down the hand. The target drops low and backs out of the head hold.	• Tuck chin. • Create leverage. • Drop low. • Back out of head hold.
Step 2 Partner drill	The assailant grabs the target's neck from behind in a one-arm head hold. The target must immediately protect the throat by tucking his or her chin into the nook of the assailant's elbow (see figure 3.9a).	Turn chin into nook of elbow.
Step 3 Partner drill	The target then creates a leverage maneuver by placing the palm of his or her hand under the assailant's elbow and grabbing the assailant's hands with a free hand. The target pushes up the assailant's elbow and pulls down on the assailant's hands (see figure 3.9b).	• Palm under elbow • Grab hand. • Push up. • Pull down.
Step 4 Partner drill	The target performs a leverage maneuver while dropping low and moving backward (see figure 3.9c). It is critical that the target drops down as low as possible (to the level of the assailant's knees) as he or she moves out of the head hold (see figure 3.9d).	• Push up. • Pull down. • Drop low.
Step 5 Partner drill	The intended target completes full motion and moves quickly away from the assailant.	• Drop low. • Move backward. • Move quickly away.
Step 6 Partner drill	Prior to the release, the intended target performs a downward kick on the assailant's instep while executing a safety yell. This will cause a distraction that will loosen the assailant's grip.	• Kick and safety yell • Tuck. • Push up. • Pull down. • Drop low and run.

Figure 3.9 *(a)* Target tucks his chin into the nook of an assailant's elbow, *(b)* target pushes up the assailant's elbow and pulls down the hand, *(c)* target drops low and backward, and *(d)* target moves out of the hold.

Variations

In a single-arm head hold, the target has both arms and both legs free. Students can experiment using their arms for a prerelease attack. They can use their hands to deliver a strike to the groin or to the eyes. They can direct the elbow to the solar plexus or groin. They can use their legs to kick the assailant's instep or knees.

Front Choke Release

Focus

The front choke is a potentially dangerous and deadly attack. A victim will lose consciousness quickly; therefore, the technique must be done efficiently and effectively. As with all releases, students must adhere to all safety rules while performing this release.

Objectives

Students will be able to do the following:

1. Execute a release from the front choke position and move quickly away from the attacker.
2. Demonstrate using their free hands or legs as potential weapons in a prerelease attack.
3. Execute a safety yell with the leg or hand strike.
4. Cooperate with a partner, adhering to all safety rules.
5. Identify the contact points needed to assist in the front choke release.

Equipment and Facilities

Gym

Front Choke Release

Organization	Extensions	Refinement cues
Step 1 Teacher demonstration	Introduction to the front choke release: To defend him- or herself from a front choke, the intended target must be aware of time. Loss of consciousness will happen quickly. The target protects the neck by dropping the chin so that the shoulders are touching the ears and extending the dominant or free arm upward. As the target steps back and away into a low horse stance, he or she brings the elbow down on the assailant's arm to break the hold.	• Scrunch. • Shoulder to ear • Step back and elbow down.
Step 2 Partner drill	Assailant stands in front of the intended target and places hands around his or her neck. The target must press down his or her chin to the neck in a scrunching motion (see figure 3.10a). The target bends his or her knees and gets ready to move. Note: Some students will be very sensitive to this attack. Assailant can place hands on the target's shoulders rather than on the neck.	• Scrunch. • Bend knees.
Step 3 Partner drill	The target extends the dominant or free arm upward, trying to bring the arm up as close as possible to the ear (see figure 3.10b).	Shoulder to ear
Step 4 Partner drill	The assailant's fingers are the weakest body part. The target must take full advantage of this vulnerability. The target now steps back and away from his or her assailant into a horse stance. As the target steps backward and away, he or she forcibly drives the extended arm downward so that the armpit is over the assailant's fingers, leading with the elbow (see figure 3.10c). A safety yell should be executed at this point.	• Shoulder to ear • Armpit over fingers • Horse stance • Elbow down • Safety yell
Step 5 Partner drill	As the target brings the elbow down, he or she will automatically be in a position to run. It is advisable in most situations to try to get away.	Run.

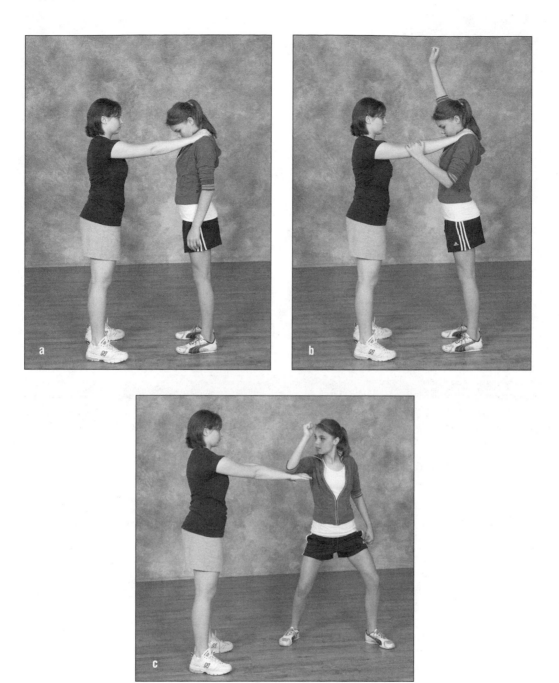

Figure 3.10   *(a)* The target in a front choke hold, *(b)* target extends her dominant arm up next to her ear, and *(c)* target steps back and away while bringing her arm down, leading with her elbow.

Variations

In many cases, it may be too difficult to escape from the choke hold. Students can experiment using their arms and legs for a prerelease attack to distract the assailant. They can perform a heel-of-palm strike, eye attack, back fist strike, or upward elbow strike with their arms. They can use their legs to deliver a kick to the knee or the groin. It is advisable to focus on the eyes and groin.

Rear Choke Release

Focus

The rear choke also presents a life-or-death situation, so a target's response must be quick and efficient. Students will learn how to successfully perform the rear choke release and escape.

Objectives

Students will be able to do the following:

1. Execute a rear choke release successfully.
2. Execute a safety yell at the moment of release.
3. Cooperate with a partner, adhering to all safety rules.
4. Identify the contact points needed to assist in the rear choke release.

Equipment and Facilities

Gym

Rear Choke Release

Organization	Extensions	Refinement cues
Step 1 Teacher demonstration	Introduction to rear choke release: This release is performed when the target is being choked from behind. The target must first scrunch down by tucking the chin and raising the shoulders. The target steps forward and brings the dominant arm up, then turns toward the raised arm and brings it down, leading with the elbow.	• Scrunch. • Step forward. • Raise arm. • Turn. • Arm down leading with elbow
Step 2 Partner drill	Assailant stands behind the target and places hands around neck. The target must first tuck the chin to the neck, or "scrunch." The target bends the knees and gets ready to move (see figure 3.11a).	• Scrunch. • Bend knees.
Step 3 Partner drill	The weakest point of the grab is the assailant's fingers. The intended target must fully concentrate on releasing the assailant's fingers. The target brings his or her arm straight up, holding it as close as possible to the ear (see figure 3.11b).	Shoulder to ear
Step 4 Partner drill	The target steps forward with the foot of opposition (e.g., if the right arm is up, then the left foot is forward) and twists toward the extended arm to face the assailant. The target brings his or her armpit over the assailant's grasp, then brings the elbow down in a continuous movement (see figure 3.11c). A safety yell is executed during the elbow movement.	• Shoulder to ear • Step. • Elbow down • Safety yell
Step 5 Partner drill	The target must maintain his or her balance, quickly back up, and then move away at the release.	• Shoulder to ear • Step. • Elbow down • Back up quickly and move away.

Variation

A variation of this technique is to bring the downward moving elbow into the chamber position, and then deliver a heel-of-palm strike, a back fist strike, or full punch to the nose (see figure 3.11d). A kick can be delivered to the groin area.

Figure 3.11 *(a)* Target in a rear choke hold, *(b)* target brings her arm straight up near her ear, *(c)* target brings elbow down in a continuous movement, and *(d)* target performs a palm heel strike on the assailant.

▶ Part 4 ◀
Activities and Handouts

Introductory Lesson
Self-Defense Questionnaire

Focus
► Active sharing of knowledge
► Introduction of unit and class procedures
► Three factors necessary for crime to occur

Objectives
Students will be able to do the following:

1. Complete the Active Knowledge Sharing assignment and discuss the answers at the end of the activity.
2. Identify the three factors necessary for crime to occur: desire, ability, and opportunity.

Equipment and Facilities
► Gym
► Handouts
  • Self-Defense Questionnaire, page 78
  • Crime-Prevention Tips, page 79

Part 1: Active Knowledge Sharing
This activity helps students to instantly connect with the subject matter. You can also use it to assess their knowledge level. It promotes teamwork, knowledge, sharing, and immediate learning.

Procedure

1. Compose a list of questions relating to self-defense. The following is a list of potential questions and answers:

   ► What two areas of the body should you strike if you are in immediate bodily danger?
   Answer: The eyes and groin are the most vulnerable, and striking them can cause the greatest injury.

   ► What should be your first reaction if you receive an obscene phone call?
   Answer: Hanging up is your first line of defense.

   ► You are alone shopping and think you are being followed. What should you do?
   Answer: Go into a store and tell the clerk that you are being followed.

   ► Which should you do first, talk to a potential attacker or resist?
   Answer: If bodily injury is imminent, you should do everything to resist. However, you can sometimes defuse a situation if you remain calm and talk with the potential attacker. Your anger can escalate the situation. Resist only as long as it is safe for you to do so. If resistance proves to be dangerous, stop.

   ► Should you carry a weapon? Are they practical?
   Answer: In general, you should not rely on weapons and they are not practical. They are not always accessible and they can be easily taken away and used against you.

▶ Should you scream if you are attacked?

Answer: Screaming can help you in some situations, especially if there are people nearby who can hear the scream. However, in some situations, such as if you are being physically held, screaming can result in bodily injury. The attacker may hit you to stop the scream.

▶ When leaving your home for the day, how can you protect it?

Answer: Lock all entrances to your home. Leave a light on. Leave a radio playing. Take in the mail.

▶ Do most victims of rape know their assailants?

Answer: Yes, approximately 73% of women are acquainted with their assailants.

▶ If you are using public transportation, what is one way you can keep yourself safe?

Answer: Wait for buses or light rail trains at stops that are well lit. If possible, join other people at a nearby stop. Try to sit toward the front near the driver. Notice whether others get off at your stop and be sure you aren't followed home.

2. Small class: Ask students to walk around the room and work on the questions together. Encourage them to discuss the questions with a variety of individuals.

   Large class: Divide class into groups of four or five. Distribute questions to each group. One student in each group should read the questions and the group should attempt to answer.

3. When the activity is finished, ask students to read each question and obtain the class's opinion on the correct answer. Allow all views to be expressed and heard.

4. Give feedback about each question, and note the ways in which the class worked out the assignment.

5. Emphasize that positive teamwork skills are necessary for success in the course.

Part 2

Facilitate a class discussion on the factors necessary for crime to occur. Use the following information to help with your class discussion.

Teacher's Resource

Potential criminals must have the following three factors in order to commit a crime: desire, ability, and opportunity. Although students cannot control an individual's desire and ability to commit a crime, if they are alert and follow simple crime-prevention rules, they can significantly reduce the opportunity for the crime to occur.

Elaborate on each topic and distribute handout (Crime-Prevention Tips).

Self-Defense Questionnaire

1. What two areas of the body should you strike if you are in immediate bodily danger?

2. What should be your first reaction if you receive an obscene phone call?

3. You are alone shopping and think you are being followed. What should you do?

4. Which should you do first, talk to the potential attacker or resist?

5. Should you carry a weapon? Are they practical?

6. Should you scream if you are attacked?

7. When leaving your home for the day, how can you protect it?

8. Do most victims of rape know their assailants?

9. If you are using public transportation, what is one way to keep yourself safe?

From J. Neide, 2009, *Teaching Self-Defense in Secondary Physical Education* (Champaign, IL: Human Kinetics).

Crime-Prevention Tips

In an emergency, dial 911

Three factors must be present for crime to occur: desire, ability, and opportunity. While citizens may not be able to change an individual's desire and ability to commit a crime, they can significantly reduce that person's opportunity by following simple crime-prevention rules.

Crime is prevented when citizens develop good habits that take away the opportunity for criminals to operate.

At Home

- ▶ Use your door viewer before opening your door.
- ▶ Secure your home before leaving it. Unless it is used, the world's best lock is useless.
- ▶ Don't hide your house key under mats, over doors, or in flower pots.
- ▶ Use interior and exterior lighting to discourage unwanted visitors.
- ▶ Have keys ready in your hand for fast entry to your home.
- ▶ Report suspicious loiterers in your neighborhood to the police.
- ▶ Place identification markers on all property. Most burglars will not steal marked property.
- ▶ If you know people who live alone, remind them not to list their addresses in the telephone directory.
- ▶ Demand identification before admitting sales or repair people, especially if you were not expecting them.
- ▶ Leave the bathroom light on while sleeping or away at night. A lit bathroom light gives the impression that someone is home and up, which can deter a burglar.

Walking

- ▶ Plan your route ahead of time, and never walk alone at night. Arrange to walk with a friend or a dog.
- ▶ Use well-lit streets, not dark alleys or bushy areas.
- ▶ Carry signaling devices like shrill alarms, shriek alarms, or a whistle to summon help in case of attack.
- ▶ Be alert! Look over your shoulder occasionally.
- ▶ Never ask for or accept rides from strangers.
- ▶ Avoid displaying or carrying large amounts of money.
- ▶ Avoid wearing or displaying valuable jewelry in public.
- ▶ Don't resist an armed robber. Hand over whatever is demanded quickly and quietly. Your life and safety are worth more than your personal effects.

(continued)

From J. Neide, 2009, Teaching Self-Defense in Secondary Physical Education (Champaign, IL: Human Kinetics).

Backpack Protection

▶ Make sure that all pockets are zipped and secured.

▶ Carry your keys, wallet, and other valuables in coat or pants pockets.

▶ Carry only minimal amounts of cash and few credit cards. Keep a record of card numbers in a safe location in your home in case your cards are lost or stolen.

▶ Know where your backpack is at all times.

Purse Protection

▶ If possible, don't carry a purse.

▶ Carry your purse against the front of your body, with your forearm across the front of the purse and your elbow held tightly against your side.

▶ Carry your keys, wallet, and other valuables in coat or pants pockets.

▶ Carry only minimal amounts of cash and few credit cards. Keep a record of card numbers in a safe location in your home in case your cards are lost or stolen.

▶ Carry the purse over your shoulder, and wear a coat over the purse if possible.

▶ Don't let your purse hang loosely in your hand. Doing so invites a thief to grab it.

▶ Never carry anything you can't afford to lose in your purse. If a purse carrying valuables is snatched, you may want to fight to keep it. It's better to surrender your purse than to fight for it.

Driving

▶ Always look inside your car before entering.

▶ Make sure all doors are locked before starting the car.

▶ Never pick up hitchhikers.

▶ If a stranger approaches while you are in your car, keep your windows closed, your door locked, and the engine running.

▶ Install a trunk release button inside the car.

▶ Engrave automobile stereo systems with your driver's license number before installation.

▶ Remember to park in well-lit areas at night.

▶ Keep the ignition key with you at all times.

▶ Lock all doors when leaving your car.

▶ Use your garage.

▶ Protect tires and rims with wheel locks.

▶ Consider using a good automobile burglar alarm system.

▶ Use locking gas caps or antisiphon screens.

▶ Don't leave valuables in your car. Put them in the trunk or cover them if you don't have a trunk.

Call the police immediately if you are attacked. Ask witnesses to stay until the police arrive.

From J. Neide, 2009, *Teaching Self-Defense in Secondary Physical Education* (Champaign, IL: Human Kinetics).

Fun Beginning

Identifying Ways People Commit Crimes

Focus

Introduce the self-defense unit by allowing students to be creative with some important self-defense topics.

Objectives

Students will be able to identify ways that people have the opportunity to commit a crime.

Equipment and Facilities

Gym

Fun Beginning

Procedure

1. Explain to students that you want to do a fun opening exercise with them before getting serious about the subject matter.

2. Divide the class into groups. Ask them to develop a list of the most effective ways to have a

   a. backpack stolen

   b. car stolen from a parking lot

   c. bicycle stolen from home

   d. wallet stolen out of your back pocket

   Deliberately ask them to make fun of the important topic you are teaching.

3. Invite the groups to present their method for committing a crime.

4. Ask students what they learned about the subject matter from this exercise. What opportunities allowed for a crime to occur?

Design an Ad Campaign for School Safety

Focus

Bring out your students' creative side by asking them to design an ad campaign for school safety.

Objectives

Students will be able to do the following:

1. Use their creativity to create an ad campaign for school safety.
2. Identify places in the school that crime could occur.
3. Identify ways to reduce crime at school.

Equipment and Facilities

▶ Gym
▶ Poster paper
▶ Colored markers

Instructions

1. Divide the class into teams of no more than five.
2. Ask the teams to design an ad campaign for school safety.
3. Teams should first discuss their school's safety issues, and then select one issue for the assignment.
4. The ad campaign must have a slogan and visual applications.
5. Before beginning the activity, discuss the characteristics of some well-known ad campaigns for safety with the teams (e.g., Smokey the Bear, Take a Bite Out of Crime).
6. Ask teams to present their ad campaigns and posters to the class.

Home Safety

Note-Taking Activity

Focus

Teach students how to secure a home and the surrounding area. Ask students to identify the key components of home safety on a handout during the lecture.

Objectives

Students will be able to do the following:

1. Recognize the ways to secure the home and surrounding area.
2. Identify the key components of home safety.

Equipment and Facilities

▶ Gym
▶ Handout: Home Safety, page 86
▶ Overhead projector
▶ Pencils

Part 1

Discuss the crime statistics for your area with your students. Information about your area is available on the Internet from your local police department or the United States crime report on the Department of Justice Web site. Note that burglary in residential areas and car theft are the two most frequent crimes. Use this statistic to segue to the home safety activity.

Part 2

Procedure

1. Distribute the Home Safety handout to the students. Use the handout as an outline for the lecture on home safety. Students should fill in the blanks as you discuss home safety.
2. Prepare overheads that show various locks for doors.
3. Discuss the pros and cons for each lock.
4. Prepare overhead transparencies describing ways to secure doors.
5. Discuss the various ways to secure doors and their price ranges.
6. Discuss various available alarm systems.
7. Discuss the use of a watchdog.
8. Discuss safety measures for outside the home, including lighting and landscaping.

Home Safety

Answer Sheet and Lecture Outline

1. Dead bolts provide more protection and slow down burglars more than other types of locks.
2. The bad feature of a dead bolt is that you need a key. In case of a fire, for example, the key must be readily available.
3. Window decals indicating that the house has an alarm system can deter burglars.
4. Use a homemade or purchased doorstop as an inexpensive way to secure your door. Cut a piece of wood to wedge between the door and a wall. The board can either be cut straight or at an angle.
5. Secure a sliding door by placing a piece of wood or metal in the track.
6. Secure windows and doors with nails or metal pins. However, drill holes into the frames so that you can remove the pins or nails in case of a fire.
7. Windows at ground level can be secured with grillwork, but it prevents escape during fire. If you use grillwork, install a safety release on the inside of the windows.
8. Do not use grillwork if you have small children at home.
9. Secure both sides of a garage door. Make sure that the inside door is very secure.
10. Remember the factors necessary for crime to occur: desire, ability, and opportunity.
11. A burglar needs the opportunity to enter as well as to escape.
12. A fence or hedge can slow down the burglar's path of escape.
13. Intruders like to conceal themselves. Trim bushes around windows so intruders do not have a place to hide.

When You Go Out

14. The best light to leave on in your home when you are gone overnight or sleeping is the bathroom light. A bathroom light shining during the night gives the impression that someone is home and awake.
15. Leave the radio or TV playing when you go out so an intruder will think that someone is at home.

What If an Intruder Comes While You Are Away?

16. If you come home and believe someone has broken into the house, do not go inside.
17. Call the police from a friend's phone. When they come, do not touch anything inside or around the house.

What If an Intruder Comes While You Are Home?

18. Make noise and turn on lights to make intruders aware they have been seen or heard.
19. If the intruder does not leave, get out of the house and go to a safe place.

(continued)

From J. Neide, 2009, Teaching Self-Defense in Secondary Physical Education (Champaign, IL: Human Kinetics).

Alarm Systems

20. Good alarms scare the intruder with noise and light.

21. One of the best alarm systems is a dog. A watchdog protects your home from unwanted intruders, but it may also cause a danger to others. There are many simulated dog alarm models, including motion, noise, and vibration sensors.

22. Alarm systems can be installed by the homeowner or a professional contractor. Check with the local police for advice on how to avoid false alarms. Calling the police with a false alarm has become a national problem.

Caution With Phones

23. Never give personal information over the phone. Never let a stranger in the house to use the phone.

24. You should not list your address in the phone book.

Walking

25. Always walk in well-lit areas.

26. Always walk against the flow of traffic.

From J. Neide, 2009, Teaching Self-Defense in Secondary Physical Education (Champaign, IL: Human Kinetics).

Home Safety

Please fill in the blanks during the class lecture.

1. _____ provide more protection and slow down burglars more than other types of locks.

2. The bad feature of this lock is that you need a _____ .

3. Window _____ indicating that the house has an alarm system can deter burglars.

4. Use a _____ as an inexpensive way to secure your door.

5. Secure a_____ by placing a piece of wood or metal in the track.

6. Secure windows and doors with _____ or _____ .

7. Windows at ground level can be secured with grillwork, but this method prevents _____

_____ .

8. Do not use grillwork if you have _____ .

9. Secure both sides of a garage door. Make sure that the _____ door is very secure.

10. Remember the factors necessary for crime to occur: _____ ,

_____ , and _____ .

11. A burglar needs the opportunity to enter as well as _____ .

12. A fence or _____ can slow down a burglar's path of escape.

13. Intruders like to conceal themselves. Trim _____ around windows so intruders do not have a place to hide.

When You Go Out

14. The best light to leave on in your home when you are gone overnight or sleeping is the _____

_____ .

15. When you go out, leave the _____ or _____ playing to fool a potential intruder.

What If an Intruder Comes While You Are Away?

16. If you come home and believe someone has broken into the house, do not _____ .

17. After you call the police from a friend's phone, you must not _____ .

What If the Intruder Comes When You Are Home?

18. Make _____ and turn on lights to make intruders aware that they have been seen or heard.

19. If the intruder does not leave, _____ and

_____ .

(continued)

From J. Neide, 2009, Teaching Self-Defense in Secondary Physical Education (Champaign, IL: Human Kinetics).

Alarm Systems

20. Good alarms scare the intruder with _____ and

    _____ .

21. One of the best alarm systems is a _____ .

22. Alarm systems can be installed by the homeowner or professionally contracted for installation. Check
    with the local _____ for advice. _____

    _____has become a national problem.

Phone Safety

23. Never give personal information over the phone. Never let _____

    _____ in the home to use the phone.

24. You should not list your _____ in the phone book.

Walking

25. Always walk in _____ areas.

26. Always walk _____ traffic.

From J. Neide, 2009, *Teaching Self-Defense in Secondary Physical Education* (Champaign, IL: Human Kinetics).

Escaping From a House Fire

Focus

Students will plan out escape routes for their own homes and learn basic rules for protecting themselves in case of a house fire. Give students a checklist on fire safety to take home for their parents or guardians.

Objectives

Students will be able to do the following:

1. Identify the key steps to escape from a house fire.
2. Design escape plans for their homes with at least two ways of exiting a room.
3. Share a checklist on fire safety with their parents or guardians.

Equipment and Facilities

▶ Paper and pencils
▶ Handouts:
  • Fire Safety, page 89
  • Is Your House Safe From Fire?, page 90
▶ Overhead projector

Part 1

Teach students the basic steps for escaping from a house fire. Introduce eight basic steps through a lecture and discussion format. Create a lecture using the information provided.

Part 2

Ask students to draw a floor plan of their homes (all floors). Students should mark two escape routes for each room; the first way out is the door. Discuss the floor plans in class and ask students to share them with their parents or guardians. Use the following list as a basis for the lecture.

Teacher Resource

Fire Safety

1. Get out fast. Never hide or take time to gather your belongings.
2. Fires are loud, hot, and smoky. The rooms and hallways will get dark very fast. You must have an escape plan. A good escape plan has two ways to get out of each room in the home. If one path is blocked by the fire, use the second route.
3. When escaping, stay low to the floor. Smoke rises during a fire. The safest air is near to the ground.
4. Feel doors before opening them for signs of heat. Begin at the bottom and then work your hands up the door. A hot door means there may be a fire on the other side. Try to get out another way.
5. If your home has security bars on the windows, every member of your family must know how to open them.
6. Choose a safe and memorable meeting place outside for your family to gather after you get out.
7. Once you are outside, call 911 or the fire department.
8. Stay away from the house no matter what. Don't go back inside for anything.

Information presented on this Web site is considered public information and may be distributed or copied. Use of appropriate byline/photo/image credits is requested. http://www.firesafety.gov/about/privacy.shtm.

Part 3

Distribute the Fire Safety checklist and ask students to fill out the Is Your House Safe From Fire? questionnaire with their parents or guardians and return it during the next class.

Fire Safety

1. Get out fast.
2. Have an escape route.
3. Stay low to the floor.
4. Check to see if the door is hot.
5. Know how to open the security bars.
6. Have a safe meeting place outside.
7. Dial 911.
8. Don't go back inside.

Information presented on this Web site is considered public information and may be distributed or copied. Use of appropriate byline/photo/image credits is requested. http://www.firesafety.gov/about/privacy.shtm.

From J. Neide, 2009, Teaching Self-Defense in Secondary Physical Education (Champaign, IL: Human Kinetics).

Is Your House Safe From Fire?

Directions: Complete this checklist with parents or guardians and return it to class.

Name _____ Period _____

Parent/guardian signature_____

Please circle yes or no.

1. Does your home have a smoke and fire alarm on each floor?	Yes	No
2. Do you have a fire extinguisher on every level of your home?	Yes	No
3. Do you have a fire extinguisher in your garage?	Yes	No
4. Does the top floor of your home have a carbon monoxide alarm?	Yes	No
5. Do you check the batteries in your smoke and fire alarm monthly?	Yes	No
6. Do your electrical outlets have two cords plugged into them at most?	Yes	No
7. Are all of the electrical outlets in your home free from dangling cords?	Yes	No
8. Do the cords on any of your appliances show signs of wear and tear?	Yes	No
9. Are any electrical cords placed under rugs or tacked to floors or walls?	Yes	No
10. Are flames guarded well in your house? (For example, does the fireplace have a screen and do the candles have holders?)	Yes	No
11. Are matches and lighters stored away from small children?	Yes	No
12. Are all flammable liquids in your home stored in airtight containers?	Yes	No
13. Are all gasoline containers stored outside of your home?	Yes	No
14. Are newspapers and oily rags properly disposed of?	Yes	No
15. In the kitchen, are your potholders, towels, and other flammable items away from the stove?	Yes	No
16. Do you leave the kitchen while you have food frying or broiling?	Yes	No
17. Do you keep a fire extinguisher in the kitchen?	Yes	No

Information presented on this Web site is considered public information and may be distributed or copied. Use of appropriate byline/photo/image credits is requested. http://www.firesafety.gov/about/privacy.shtm.

From J. Neide, 2009, Teaching Self-Defense in Secondary Physical Education (Champaign, IL: Human Kinetics).

Internet Safety

Focus

Students will learn simple steps for discouraging Internet intruders, as well as what to do if problems continue to occur. After the lecture, give students a handout that summarizes the major points but omits some key terms. Ask the students to fill in the blanks, and then discuss the answers with the whole class.

Objectives

Students will be able to do the following:

1. Identify key points for discouraging Internet intruders.
2. Demonstrate their knowledge in class.
3. Participate in a discussion on Internet intruders and safety.

Equipment and Facilities

▶ Classroom or gym
▶ Overhead projector
▶ Handout: Internet Safety, page 94
▶ Pencils

Part 1

Create a handout summarizing key points for computer safety. Instead of providing a complete text, leave portions of it blank with answers scrambled below. After completing the lecture-based presentation, students fill out the questionnaire.

Part 2

Use the following information to create a lecture-based presentation on computer safety.

Staying Safe Online

Everyone should know the following precautionary steps before using the computer. The benefits of computers are immeasurable, but computer users must beware of scam artists, viruses, spam, and content that is inappropriate for children. Certain precautions can help protect against these unwanted dangers.

Microsoft suggests the following steps:

Protecting Your PC or Mac

1. Use an Internet firewall.
2. Make sure your operating system and software are up-to-date.
3. Install antivirus software and update it regularly.

Reduce Exposure to Spam

1. Use e-mail filtering tools.
2. Report spammers to your e-mail service provider.
3. Be vigilant when giving out your primary e-mail address. Never respond to spam.

Protect Against Internet Scams

1. Don't give out personal information unless you trust the Web site.
2. Never give out your password.
3. Only distribute your credit card numbers on secure Web sites. Never send this information in an e-mail or instant message. Use the privacy and security options available on your Internet browser.

Reference: microsoft.com.

Additional items to cover:

1. Do not open e-mail attachments that are programs (the file name will be .exe).
2. Do not open e-mails if you do not know the sender.
3. Always scan programs and files you download from the Internet with an antivirus program. Select files to download carefully.

Part 3

At the conclusion of the lecture, distribute the handout (see Internet Safety, page 94) to the students. Explain that you have left out some key terms, and ask them to fill in the blanks.

Part 4

After the students have completed the handout, discuss the correct answers with the group.

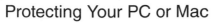

Internet Safety Answer Sheet for Teachers

Protecting Your PC or Mac

1. Use an Internet firewall.
2. Make sure your operating system and software are up-to-date.
3. Install antivirus software and update it regularly.

Reduce Exposure to Spam

1. Use e-mail filtering tools.
2. Report spammers to your e-mail service provider.
3. Be vigilant when giving out your primary e-mail address. Never respond to spam.

Protect Against Internet Scams

1. Don't give out personal information unless you trust the Web site.
2. Never give out your password.
3. Only distribute your credit card numbers on secure Web sites. Never send this information in an e-mail or instant message. Use the privacy and security options available on your Internet browser.

From J. Neide, 2009, Teaching Self-Defense in Secondary Physical Education (Champaign, IL: Human Kinetics).

Internet Safety

Fill in the blank spaces with the correct answer. Answers can be found in the list below.

Protecting your PC or Mac

1. Use an Internet _____.
2. Make sure your operating system and software are _____.
3. Install _____ software and update it regularly.

Reduce Exposure to Spam

1. Use e-mail _____ tools.
2. Report _____ to your e-mail service provider.
3. Be vigilant when giving out your primary _____ address. Never respond to spam.

Protect Against Internet Scams

1. Don't give out personal information unless you _____ the Web site.
2. Never give out your _____.
3. Only distribute your credit card numbers on secure Web sites. Never send this information in an _____ or _____.
4. Use the privacy and _____ options available on your Internet browser.

Answer List

up-to-date	password
filtering	spammers
trust	antivirus
firewall	e-mail
instant message	security

From J. Neide, 2009, Teaching Self-Defense in Secondary Physical Education (Champaign, IL: Human Kinetics).

Deescalating a Potential Confrontation

Focus

Students are confronted daily with situations that could escalate into an unsafe conflict. Show students how situations can escalate into confrontation. Ask them to practice deescalating a confrontation through several role-playing scenarios.

Objectives

Students will be able to do the following:

1. Determine how their spoken and body languages can escalate situations.
2. Demonstrate how to deescalate several potential confrontations through role playing.

Equipment and Facilities

- ▶ Gym
- ▶ Chairs
- ▶ Handouts: Deescalation Task Sheets, pages 96-98
- ▶ Pencils

Part 1: Escalating a Situation

We have the potential to escalate or deescalate the situation in every encounter. The following lesson examines how situations can be escalated or deescalated by our behaviors, both verbal and nonverbal.

Situations can be escalated when participants use threatening gestures and words, ignore others, make unkind remarks, shout, invade others' space, and use obscenities.

Begin the lesson by demonstrating a variety of situations that could happen to a student. Use bodily and verbal behavior that escalates the situation. Discuss how and why the demonstrated situation escalated.

Scenarios

Here are examples for teachers to demonstrate with a student that would show verbal and bodily behavior that escalates the situation. The teacher should do the opposite of the behavior suggested on the task sheet.

1. The student complains to a teacher about a grade he or she has received.
2. Teacher disciplines a student for his or her behavior in the classroom.

Part 2: Deescalation

Provide task sheets with three new situations for the students to act out. Explain the procedures to the students and place them in groups of three. Each scenario calls for an assailant, a victim, and a recorder, and each student should play each role during the course of the three scenarios. Students should return the task sheet when finished. If groups finish early, they may practice previously learned releases until the entire class is finished. Review the main points of deescalating potential confrontations with the class.

Deescalation Task Sheet

Victim _____

Assailant _____

Recorder _____

Work in groups of three. Take turns acting as victim, assailant, and recorder. Each person should play each role by the end of the exercise. While the victim and assailant play out the scene, the recorder observes and writes down the victim's verbal and body language.

Chair Confrontation

The assailant sits in a chair. The victim approaches the assailant and asks to have the seat. The assailant initially refuses to give up the seat. The victim must either convince the assailant to give up the seat or come up with a reasonable solution to the problem.

When you are finished, return to your group and practice previously learned releases.

Victim's verbal and body language	Yes	No
Maintains eye contact		
Neutral facial expression		
Posture erect and ready but calm		
Confident stance		
Distance of 2 arm lengths		
Clear in speech and moderate in tone		
Listens		
Acknowledges feelings		
Communicates clearly		
Doesn't confront or verbally attack person		

From J. Neide, 2009, Teaching Self-Defense in Secondary Physical Education (Champaign, IL: Human Kinetics).

Deescalation Task Sheet

Victim _____

Assailant _____

Recorder _____

Work in groups of three. Take turns acting as victim, assailant, and recorder. Each person should play each role by the end of the exercise. While the victim and assailant play out the scene, the recorder observes and writes down the victim's verbal and body language.

Bumped in the Hallway

Victim pretends to walk down a hallway. The assailant bumps into the victim and says, "Watch out." The victim is now confronted by the assailant, who wants to show the other students in the hallway that he or she is in control.

When you are finished, return to your group and practice previously learned releases.

Victim's verbal and body language	Yes	No
Maintains eye contact		
Neutral facial expression		
Posture erect and ready but calm		
Confident stance		
Distance of 2 arm lengths		
Clear in speech and moderate in tone		
Listens		
Acknowledges feelings		
Communicates clearly		
Doesn't confront or verbally attack person		

From J. Neide, 2009, Teaching Self-Defense in Secondary Physical Education (Champaign, IL: Human Kinetics).

Deescalation Task Sheet

Victim _____

Assailant _____

Recorder _____

Work in groups of three. Take turns acting as victim, assailant, and recorder. Each person should play each role by the end of the exercise. While the victim and assailant play out the scene, the recorder observes and writes down the victim's verbal and body language.

Missing Pen

The victim thinks that his or her pen has been taken by a student. The victim confronts the assailant, who has taken the pen and will not return it.

When you are finished, return to your group and practice previously learned releases.

Victim's verbal and body language	Yes	No
Maintains eye contact		
Neutral facial expression		
Posture erect and ready but calm		
Confident stance		
Distance of 2 arm lengths		
Clear in speech and moderate in tone		
Listens		
Acknowledges feelings		
Communicates clearly		
Doesn't confront or verbally attack person		

From J. Neide, 2009, Teaching Self-Defense in Secondary Physical Education (Champaign, IL: Human Kinetics).

Contact Points

Focus

Students will learn to identify contact points that are used with self-defense techniques. They will trace their own outlines on paper and tape them to the wall to visualize the weak points of the body.

Objectives

Students will be able to do the following:

1. Cooperate with their partners to trace body outlines.
2. Identify contact points on an anatomical drawing.
3. Demonstrate directing hand and foot attacks to contact points.

Equipment and Facilities

- ▶ 3-by-6-foot (1 by 2 m) sheet of paper for each student or group
- ▶ Pencils or markers
- ▶ Tape
- ▶ Handout: Contact Points, page 101
- ▶ Anatomical chart (optional)

Part 1

Create a lecture on the contact points using the following information.

The following list (Tedeschi 2003) about the human body represents the contact points that are used in self-defense. Damage to the weak points can cause trauma to blood vessels, nerves, bones, tissue, and joints. The level of damage during an attack depends on the force, angle, method, and hitting technique used, as well as the composition of the assailant's body. In martial arts, the number of contact points on the human body can reach 108 points, but basic self-defense focuses on fewer areas. In all attacks, the victim's main goal is to prevent the attacker from moving forward or seeing.

Head Area

- ▶ Eyes: Strikes to the eye can result in corneal abrasion, retinal detachment, global rupture, or fracture of the socket.
- ▶ Nose: The nose is structurally weakest on the sides, so a side hit will cause the greatest damage, but a frontal hit can also be very effective and painful. When struck on the nose, the assailant's eyes will tear up and momentarily lose vision.
- ▶ Chin: As with the nose, hitting the chin sideways will cause the most damage. With enough force, the TMJ (joint) will fracture at the back of the mandible.
- ▶ Neck: Strikes to the neck should be directed to the major blood vessels, the carotid and jugular. Choking the neck and closing these blood vessels will restrict blood flow to the brain, resulting in a loss of consciousness or even death. Hitting the sides of the neck can damage nerves and dislocate the adjacent cervical vertebrae, which impairs motor functions. A strike to the larynx and trachea can obstruct the airway and cause bleeding into the throat. This injury can cause death.

Shoulder Area

Collarbone: A downward strike easily fractures the collarbone, but this injury will not incapacitate the assailant. Strikes to the collarbone should not be the first line of defense.

Trunk

▶ Solar plexus: The solar plexus is a nerve network point below the sternum. Strikes to this area will hinder breathing. Hitting the sternum with great force can damage the heart.

▶ Genitalia: Strikes to this area are very painful, but not always debilitating.

Hands

Fingers: Twisting or breaking the fingers will inflict pain and can help a victim break from a hold.

Legs and Feet

▶ Knees: The knee is the most vulnerable part of the leg and can be attacked from any direction. Damage to the knee can cause a loss of mobility. The kneecap dislocates laterally, so horizontal or 45-degree angle blows are the most efficient.

▶ Toes: A victim can easily stomp on and break an assailant's toes.

Source: Tedeschi, M. 2003. Essential Anatomy for Healing and Martial Arts. CT: Weatherhill, Inc.

Part 2

Arrange the students into groups of four. Tell them to choose one member of the group to lie down on a large piece of paper. The others should draw an outline of the student's body on the paper. After the students have completed their drawings, they should identify areas of attacking points, including the eyes, chin, nose, collarbone, trachea, larynx, sternum, solar plexus, genitalia, knees, toe joints, and fingers. Students should mark these points on the drawings and tape them to a wall.

Part 3

Demonstrate the following listed techniques on a drawing taped to the wall. Students should return to their groups and practice each technique on their drawings.

Part 4

Ask the students to form pairs within their groups. Each student should slowly and carefully go through the techniques with a partner. Caution the students to be careful and not to use force.

Target	Technique
Eyes	Finger strike or thumbs
Chin	Heel-of-palm strike upward, forward or reverse punch, elbow strike
Nose	Heel-of-palm strike, back fist strike, forward or reverse punch, elbow strike
Trachea	Finger strike, forward or reverse punch, back fist strike, elbow strike
Larynx	Finger strike, forward or reverse punch, back fist strike, elbow strike
Sternum	Forward or reverse punch, elbow strike
Solar plexus	Forward or reverse punch, elbow strike
Genitalia	Front kick, back kick, forward or reverse punch
Knee	Front kick, back kick, side kick
Toe joints	Stomp
Fingers	Grab, bend, twist

Contact Points

Target	Technique
Eyes	Finger strike or thumbs
Chin	Heel-of-palm strike upward, forward or reverse punch, side elbow strike
Nose	Heel-of-palm strike, back fist strike, forward or reverse punch, elbow strike
Trachea	Finger strike, forward or reverse punch, back fist strike, elbow strike
Larynx	Finger strike, forward or reverse punch, back fist strike, elbow strike
Sternum	Forward or reverse punch, elbow strike
Solar plexus	Forward or reverse punch, elbow strike
Genitalia	Front kick, back kick, forward or reverse punch
Knee	Front kick, back kick, side kick
Toe joints	Stomp
Fingers	Grab, bend, twist

From J. Neide, 2009, Teaching Self-Defense in Secondary Physical Education (Champaign, IL: Human Kinetics).

Self-Defense Scenarios

Focus

Students will put their new skills to use in several self-defense scenarios, in which they must either defuse the situation or use appropriate physical force. Use the grading rubric at the end of the lesson to assess student performance.

Objectives

Students will be able to do the following:

1. Analyze potentially dangerous situations and determine the best course of action.
2. Demonstrate self-defense moves that are practical and efficient for each scenario.
3. Evaluate the effectiveness of their chosen self-defense techniques.

Equipment and Facilities

- ▶ Gym
- ▶ Handout: Self-Defense Scenarios (two-week unit, page 104, or four-week unit, page 105)
- ▶ Chairs
- ▶ Mats
- ▶ Assessment Rubric for Self-Defense Scenarios, page 103

Part 1

Create a handout that describes several examples of potentially dangerous situations.

Part 2

Ask students to form groups of four and to act out the chosen scenarios using the following progression.

1. Move slowly, paying attention to detail. The instructor should check student performance for form and validity of chosen technique.
2. Use medium speed with assailant holding on tighter (if applicable) or asserting a little more force.
3. Use medium speed with strength and verbal confrontation.
4. Use a surprise attack.

Remind students that they must pay particular attention to safety and bodily contact, and use techniques that show an escape.

Part 3

Bring the class together and discuss each group's self-defense movements. Evaluate the validity of each technique and suggest any alternative self-defense movements. Always remind students that avoidance is the key to good self-defense. Analyze whether the situation might have been prevented or defused.

Assessment Rubric for Self-Defense Scenarios

Note: The following rubric can be used for individual assessment.

A. Excellent—The student chose correct techniques, showed power, maintained good balance, and displayed an assertive attitude.

B. Strong—The student chose correct techniques and maintained good balance, but showed little power and displayed minimal assertiveness.

C. Adequate—The student chose correct technique, but hesitated and may have needed prompting. The student showed some power, maintained good balance, and displayed an acceptable attitude of assertiveness.

D. Poor—The student performed the technique after prompting from the teacher, and showed an acceptable level of power, balance, and assertiveness.

E. Fundamentally deficient—The student performed the skill incorrectly, and showed no balance, power, or assertiveness.

From J. Neide, 2009, Teaching Self-Defense in Secondary Physical Education (Champaign, IL: Human Kinetics).

Self-Defense Scenarios

Two-Week Unit (10 days)

Please form groups of four and act out the scenarios using the following progression. Please find one technique that can successfully deter the attack. Remember to maintain balance, poise, and commitment to the technique. Also remember that after delivering the technique(s), you must always be alert for a continuation of the attack.

Progressions

1. Move slowly, paying attention to detail. The instructor should check student performance for form and validity of chosen technique.
2. Use medium speed with assailant holding on tighter (if applicable) or asserting a little more force.
3. Use medium speed with strength and verbal confrontation.
4. Use a surprise attack.

Remember safety!

Situation

1. You are attacked from the front and your assailant
   a. grabs your arm and tries to force you into a car
   b. grabs your arm and tries to push you into a wall
   c. grabs both of your wrists and tries to drag you into an alley
   d. grabs both of your wrists and tries to kick you in the groin
   e. grabs one wrist with two hands and tries to pull you to the ground

2. You are attacked from behind and your assailant
   a. grabs your arm and twists you around
   b. grabs both your shoulders and shakes you violently
   c. grabs you from behind, turns you around, and attempts to hit you in the face

3. You are sitting on a chair, and the assailant grabs your arm and tries to remove you from the chair.

4. You are pushed against a wall and your assailant
   a. pins your back to the wall holding your hands
   b. holds your chest against the wall

5. You meet a stranger on the street who
   a. persistently asks you for money even after you have said, "No!"
   b. screams obscenities at you
   c. continues to talk to you until you feel uncomfortable

From J. Neide, 2009, *Teaching Self-Defense in Secondary Physical Education* (Champaign, IL: Human Kinetics).

Self-Defense Scenarios

Four-Week Unit (20 days)

Please form groups of four and act out the scenarios using the following progression. Please find one technique that can successfully deter the attack. Remember to maintain balance, poise, and commitment to the technique. Also remember that after delivering the technique(s), you must always be alert for a continuation of the attack.

Progressions

1. Move slowly, paying attention to detail.
2. Use medium speed with assailant holding on tighter (if applicable) or asserting a little more force.
3. Use medium speed with strength and verbal confrontation.
4. Use a surprise attack.

Remember safety!

Situation

1. You are attacked from the front and your assailant
   a. grabs your arm and tries to force you into a car
   b. grabs your arm and tries to push you into a wall
   c. grabs both of your wrists and tries to drag you into an alley
   d. grabs both of your wrists and tries to kick you in the groin
   e. grabs one wrist with two hands and tries to pull you to the ground
2. You are attacked from behind and your assailant
   a. pins your arms in a bear hug and lifts you up
   b. grabs your arm and twists you around
   c. grabs both your shoulders and shakes you violently
   d. grabs you from behind, turns you around, and attempts to hit you in the face
3. You are sitting on a chair and the assailant
   a. grabs your arm and tries to remove you from the chair
   b. puts you in a headlock from behind
   c. tries to choke you from behind
4. You are attacked from the front and your assailant
   a. grabs your throat and begins to choke you
   b. grabs both your arms and pins them to your body
5. You are attacked from behind and your assailant
   a. grabs your throat and tries to choke you
   b. puts you in a head hold
   c. puts your head in a full nelson
6. You are pushed against a wall and your assailant
   a. pins your back to the wall holding your hands
   b. holds your chest against the wall
7. You meet a stranger on the street who
   a. persistently asks you for money even after you have said, "No!"
   b. screams obscenities at you
   c. continues to talk to you until you feel uncomfortable

From J. Neide, 2009, *Teaching Self-Defense in Secondary Physical Education* (Champaign, IL: Human Kinetics).

Myths and Facts About Rape

What Should I Do?

Focus

This lesson is a great way to introduce the myths and facts of sexual assault. Ask students to complete a questionnaire that will help them think about the topic in a safe environment. Provide the correct answers and discuss the myths and facts of the topic. Give students instructions about what to do if they or a friend are raped.

Objectives

Students will be able to do the following:

1. Identify the main facts about rape during class discussion.
2. Participate in a discussion on sexual assault.
3. Identify the steps to take if they or a friend are raped.

Equipment and Facilities

- ▶ Gym
- ▶ Overhead projector
- ▶ Handout: Myths and Facts About Rape, page 108
- ▶ 3-by-5-inch (8 by 13 cm) cards
- ▶ Pencils

Part 1

Provide a questionnaire on the myths and facts about rape that is appropriate for the age and maturity levels of the class.

Part 2

Ask the students to complete the handout and to think about questions that they would like to have answered. Because sexual assault is a very sensitive subject, many students will not want to ask a question publicly. You can provide 3-by-5-inch (8 by 13 cm) cards for students to write down their questions privately.

Part 3

Answer student questions from discussion or the index cards. Review the procedure students should take if they or a friend have been raped. Use the following information with the overhead transparencies (pages 111 and 112) during the discussion.

Teacher's Resource

If You Are Attacked

Go with your instincts. You may decide to run, scream, kick, hit, or bite. Resist any way you think is necessary. Your goal is to escape safely. Cooperate with your assailant if you think that resisting could lead to further harm or put your life in danger. Never feel guilty about anything you did or didn't do.

If You Have Been Raped

What should you do after you get away from your attacker?

▶ Get to a safe place.

▶ Call a rape crisis hotline such as the Rape, Abuse, and Incest National Network (RAINN) at 800-656-HOPE (800-656-4673).

▶ Go to a hospital. You can get tests and treatment for any injuries. Don't bathe, brush your teeth, or change your clothing.

▶ Report the rape. This is an important step, but you should be comfortable with your decision before filing the report.

▶ Get information and support from a professional agency, such as a rape crisis center.

▶ Seek counseling. A counselor can help you deal with painful feelings about the attack.

Remember: Rape is never the victim's fault!

Myths and Facts About Rape

1.	Rape is the most frequently committed violent crime in the United States.	Agree	Disagree
2.	Rape is a minor offense. Its significance is exaggerated.	Agree	Disagree
3.	Rape happens to people of all ages, races, educational backgrounds, religions, and physical descriptions.	Agree	Disagree
4.	Most victims of rape are young.	Agree	Disagree
5.	Most victims of rape know their assailants.	Agree	Disagree
6.	About 10-20% of all sexual assaults are reported.	Agree	Disagree
7.	Rape is motivated by sudden, uncontrollable sexual urges.	Agree	Disagree
8.	Rapists rarely repeat their crime.	Agree	Disagree
9.	Rape and sexual assault occur most frequently in the victim's home.	Agree	Disagree
10.	It is not necessary for a rape victim to go to the hospital unless there is physical injury.	Agree	Disagree

From J. Neide, 2009, Teaching Self-Defense in Secondary Physical Education (Champaign, IL: Human Kinetics).

Myths and Facts About Rape

Teacher's Answer Sheet

1. Rape is the most frequently committed violent crime in the U.S.

False. Rape is an infrequent crime. The most frequently committed crimes are aggravated assault and domestic violence. According to findings from the National Crime Victimization Survey, in 2005, U.S. residents aged 12 or older were victims of approximately 23 million crimes.

- ▶ 77% (18.0 million) were property crimes.
- ▶ 22% (5.2 million) were crimes of violence.
- ▶ 1% (227,000) were personal thefts.

In 2005, for every 1,000 U.S. residents aged 12 or older, there occurred

- ▶ 1 rape or sexual assault
- ▶ 1 assault with injury
- ▶ 3 robberies

Murder is the least frequent violent crime. In 2005, there were about 6 murder victims per 100,000 persons in the United States.

Resource: RAINN (Rape, Abuse, and Incest National Network): www.rainn.org/statistics
Resource: U.S. Department of Justice www.ojp.usdoj.gov/bjs/cvictgen.htm.

2. Rape is a minor offense. Its significance is exaggerated.

False. In 2007, the FBI reported that 194,580 sexual assaults, including rape and attempted rape, occurred. This number is significant and the gravity of the crime is significant.

Resource: Department of Justice: www.fbi.gov/ucr/prelim2007/index.html.

3. Rape happens to people of all ages, races, educational levels, religions, and physical descriptions.

True. Rapists look for vulnerable persons to victimize, not simply attractive ones. People of all ages, from a 6-month-old infant to the elderly, have been victims of rape. Boys, girls, men, and women have all experienced rape. A recent study by RAINN (www.rainn.org/statistics) showed that 99% of people with physical challenges have experienced some sort of sexual assault. Most rape is intraracial (within one's own racial group), not interracial. One in six women and one in 33 men will be sexually assaulted in his or her lifetime.

4. Most victims of rape are young.

True. Anyone can be raped, but most victims of rape are between the ages of 14 and 19. Rapists target teenage girls more frequently than women in any other age group. Many of these crimes are categorized as acquaintance rape. Women between 16 and 19 years old are four times more likely to be sexually assaulted than women in other age groups.

Fifteen percent of sexual assault and rape victims are less than 12 years old. Forty-four percent are younger than 18, and 80% are younger than 30 (www.rainn.org/statistics).

5. Most victims of rape know their assailants.

True. According to RAINN (www.rainn.org/statistics), 73% of sexual assaults are committed by an acquaintance of the victim. In juvenile sexual assault cases, 34% of attackers are family members, and 59% are acquaintances.

(continued)

From J. Neide, 2009, Teaching Self-Defense in Secondary Physical Education (Champaign, IL: Human Kinetics).

6. **About 10-20% of all sexual assaults are reported.**

False. According to RAINN (www.rainn.org/statistics), 40% of sexual assaults are reported to the police. Since 1993, reporting has increased by one third.

7. **Rape is motivated by sudden, uncontrollable, sexual urges.**

False. In addition to sexual violence, rape is an act of physical and emotional violence. Rapists are more motivated by anger and the need for power than by sexual desire.

8. **Rapists rarely repeat their crime.**

False. Rapists do repeat their crime, but the majority choose a different victim. In addition, 46% of rapists released from prison were rearrested within the next 3 years for a different crime (www.rainn.org/statistics):

- ▶ 18.6% for a violent offense
- ▶ 14.8% for a property crime
- ▶ 11.2% for a drug offense
- ▶ 20.5% for a public-order offense

9. **Rape and sexual assault occur most frequently in the victim's home.**

False. However, 50% of all reported incidents of rape and sexual assault occurred within 1 mile of the victim's home. Four out of ten incidents took place in the victim's home (www.rainn.org/statistics).

10. **It is not necessary for a rape victim to go to the hospital unless there is physical injury.**

False. It is very important for victims to go to the hospital after being raped. Here are the reasons:

a. They need to see if they have any injuries. During shock, victims may not perceive injury.
b. They need to be tested for sexually transmitted diseases and pregnancy.
c. They need to seek medical evidence for future prosecution.

From J. Neide, 2009, Teaching Self-Defense in Secondary Physical Education (Champaign, IL: Human Kinetics).

What to Do If You Are Attacked

▶ Go with your instincts.

▶ Your goal is to escape safely.

Overhead—*From J. Neide, 2009, Teaching Self-Defense in Secondary Physical Education (Champaign, IL: Human Kinetics).*

If You Have Been Raped

▶ Go to a safe place.

▶ Go to a hospital.

▶ Report the rape.

▶ Seek counseling.

Overhead—*From J. Neide, 2009, Teaching Self-Defense in Secondary Physical Education (Champaign, IL: Human Kinetics).*

Acquaintance Rape and Gender Stereotyping

Focus

Students form small groups to discuss gender stereotyping and its connection to acquaintance rape. By the end of the lesson, students should understand the effects of gender stereotyping in their society and the facts about acquaintance rape.

Objectives

Students will be able to do the following:

1. Answer and identify key questions about acquaintance rape in a small group scenario assignment.
2. Define gender stereotyping for their society.
3. Cooperate with and listen to their classmates in a very frank discussion on acquaintance rape.

Equipment and Facilities

- ▶ Gym
- ▶ Overhead projector
- ▶ Handout: Acquaintance Rape Story, page 117

Part 1

Distribute the Acquaintance Rape Story handout, then ask the students to sit and read the story completely. Place the students into small groups to discuss the questions at the end of the written text.

Note: It is advisable to preassign the discussion groups for compatibility and a feeling of safety. This topic can be very sensitive for many members of the class, and each student should feel as comfortable as possible.

Part 2

Bring the class together for a discussion on acquaintance rape. Next, introduce the term *gender stereotyping* with examples on an overhead or a blackboard. Identify places in the story where the portrayal of both the boy's and girl's actions would be considered gender stereotyping.

Part 3

As class time permits, lead a discussion on stereotyping and preventive measures against rape. (See teacher's resource.)

Teacher's Resource

Stereotypical Gender Roles

Use the following list as talking points in the class discussion on stereotypical gender roles.

To Be Masculine . . .

- ▶ When you're with the guys, talk about scoring and belittle women.
- ▶ Make sexist jokes.
- ▶ Refer to women as "chicks" or "bitches."
- ▶ You should be able to support a family someday.
- ▶ Learn to fix things, work on cars, specialize in manual labor, and be self-sufficient.

- ▶ Run from commitment. Avoid relationships with women who try to tie you down.
- ▶ Check women out, rate them, and dissect them with your eyes. Only look at the outside, not the inside.
- ▶ Don't show too much emotion. Real men don't cry.
- ▶ Be strong and aggressive. When you know what you want, go for it, and don't get whipped by some woman.

To be Feminine . . .

- ▶ Don't act smart. You might intimidate a man. Women are airheads or dumb blondes, not rocket scientists.
- ▶ Women need to be taken care of and protected.
- ▶ Always strive for the perfect body. Thin is in, and any extra fat is a sign that you are not taking care of yourself.
- ▶ You must use your looks to compete for available men.
- ▶ Be emotional.
- ▶ Always take care of others and don't assert yourself.
- ▶ Women are nice and polite.
- ▶ A wedding ring is a symbol of success.
- ▶ Dress for fashion, not for comfort or safety.

Resource: O'Neal, P. (ND) Acquaintance Rape. Sacramento, CA: CSU, Sacramento Women's Resource Center.

Prevention Strategies

Use the following information when discussing prevention strategies.

Men:

- ▶ Acts of sexual intercourse with minors are unlawful. In most states, a minor is a person younger than 18 years old. Check your state law to find the legal age of consent.
- ▶ Do not believe myths such as yes means yes and no means maybe, or she says no but she really means yes.
- ▶ If you feel that your partner is giving you mixed messages, talk to her about your confusion. Allow her to clarify what she wants, but don't pressure her into changing her mind if she says, "No."
- ▶ Don't ever think that a woman owes you sex.
- ▶ Don't drink alcohol or do drugs. Alcohol and drugs will affect your behavior and your judgment.
- ▶ Think of rape and all violence against women as if it is on a continuum. Violence starts with small remarks and jokes and can escalate from there.
- ▶ Be aware of all the ways that men try to have power over women.

Women:

- ▶ Acts of sexual intercourse with minors are unlawful. In most states, a minor is a person younger than 18 years old. Check your state law to find the legal age of consent.
- ▶ Practice being assertive.
- ▶ When in doubt, say, *"No!"*
- ▶ Don't drink alcohol or do drugs. Alcohol and drugs will affect your behavior and your judgment.
- ▶ Structure your dates to be on your terms.
- ▶ Be direct!

Resource: O'Neal, P. (ND) Acquaintance Rape. Sacramento, CA: CSU, Sacramento Women's Resource Center.

Teacher's Resource

Sexual Assault

The following list presents suggestions for preventing sexual assault. Use this list as a tool for a frank and open discussion of sexual assault.

Suggestions for Prevention

1. **Know you have the right to set sexual limits.** You may have different limits with different people, but you need to know that your limits or the limits of others may change.

2. **Communicate those limits.** You must be explicit about your needs and desires. Others cannot read your mind.

3. **Trust your feelings.** Be aware of peer pressure to have sex and partners who might manipulate you into having unwanted sex.

4. **Pay attention to behaviors that don't seem right.** Be aware of the behaviors of people around you, such as these:

   a. People sitting or standing too close who appear to enjoy your discomfort.

   b. People who speak or act as if they know you intimately, but don't.

   c. People who grab or push you to get their way. This is inappropriate behavior and should not be tolerated.

   d. People who do not listen or ignore what you are saying, such as "No!"

5. **Be assertive.** It is okay to do these things:

   a. Get angry when someone does something that is not appropriate.

   b. Respond immediately with a strong response, such as yelling, hitting, or running.

   c. Stand up for your rights. It is okay to be rude to someone who is pressuring you sexually.

   d. Hurt someone's feelings.

6. **Rehearse.** Think about the steps you can take if others make you feel uncomfortable. Mentally rehearse these scenarios so that you can react more quickly.

Sexual Assault

Suggestions for Prevention

1. Know that you have the right to set sexual limits.
2. Communicate those limits.
3. Trust your feelings.
4. Pay attention to behaviors that don't seem right.
5. Be assertive.
6. Rehearse.

Overhead—*From J. Neide, 2009, Teaching Self-Defense in Secondary Physical Education (Champaign, IL: Human Kinetics).*

Acquaintance Rape Story

Tony brings Diane to a party, where he gets drunk at the encouragement of his friends. During the party, Tony keeps giving Diane beers. Diane doesn't like beer, but she drinks it anyway because she doesn't want Tony to think she's not fun. Tony makes comments about Diane's appearance, such as how nice she would look in a short skirt, but she ignores him. Tony soon becomes drunk. After a while, he tells Diane he wants to be alone with her so they can talk. Diane doesn't feel like leaving, but she goes with Tony because she wants to please him. He takes her to a deserted street and parks. They start kissing and Diane enjoys it, but in the back of her mind, she is thinking of the time when she will have to tell him that she doesn't want to go any further. Unfortunately, Tony isn't thinking about what Diane wants. He doesn't care. In fact, he can tell she is beginning to feel uncomfortable, but he is enjoying the feelings he's getting: the feeling of having power over someone. There are two voices having an argument inside Tony's head.

Voice 1

Go for it! She came with you. She knew what would happen. She might say "no," but girls always do. It's okay to do it. All the guys do. You have a right to have sex. She's leading you on and asking for it.

Voice 2

She doesn't want to go any further. She seems scared. You should take her home. It's not right to force her.

So What Did Tony Do?

Tony blocked out voice 2 (the alcohol helped). He liked the feeling of power he got from forcing Diane to have sex. He felt in control and strong; he thought he was doing what men were expected to do.

Tony raped Diane, and although he tried not to notice, he saw that she was crying. After it was all over, he just wanted to get her home. They were silent all the way to her house. As soon as they got there, Diane leapt out of the car and ran inside. They were polite to each other at school after the incident, but they never went out again.

Diane blamed herself for the whole thing. How could she have allowed herself to be alone with him? Why did she drink? Maybe if she hadn't drunk any beer, she would have had better judgment, and therefore would have never left the party alone with him. She also felt guilty about kissing him; if she hadn't been making out with him, he would never have expected her to have sex with him. Consequently, Diane was filled with self-hatred and told no one what happened.

Tony couldn't bring himself to brag to his friends about what had happened because he had seen the tears in Diane's eyes. *Maybe I shouldn't have forced her,* he thought. *Oh, well!* Tony and Diane's friends thought they stopped dating because they had a fight. Tony put the incident out of his mind, but Diane never forgot and was never the same afterward.

What Do You Think?

Please get into small groups and discuss the following questions. Be honest and listen to everyone's opinion.

- ▶ Do you think the rape was Diane's fault?
- ▶ Did Tony have a right to have sex with Diane since he thought she led him on?
- ▶ How could this rape have been prevented?

Resource: O'Neal, P. (ND) Acquaintance Rape. Sacramento, CA: CSU, Sacramento Women's Resource Center.

From J. Neide, 2009, Teaching Self-Defense in Secondary Physical Education (Champaign, IL: Human Kinetics).

Stages of Acquaintance Rape

Focus

Introduce students to the stages of acquaintance rape and ask them to read a short story on their own. Next, discuss how the stages of acquaintance rape appear in the story. Ask the students what measures could have prevented the rape or reduced the chance of assault.

Objectives

Students will be able to do the following:

1. Identify the stages of acquaintance rape.
2. Think of preventive measures that can be taken to reduce the risk of rape.

Equipment and Facilities

▶ Classroom or gym
▶ Overhead projector
▶ Handout: Scenario of Stages of Acquaintance Rape, page 120

Part 1

Teach the students about the stages of acquaintance rape using the overhead on page 119.

Teacher's Resource

Stages of Acquaintance Rape

▶ Intrusion: The rapist makes the victim feel uncomfortable with an unwanted touch or look. The rapist notices the victim's reaction and proceeds from there.
▶ Desensitization: The victim ignores the rapist's intrusions or makes excuses for them. She doesn't take the rapist seriously or thinks, *That's just the way he is.*
▶ Isolation: The rapist gets the victim alone, whether in a car, in an apartment, or outside.

Resource: O'Neal, P. (ND) Acquaintance Rape. Sacramento, CA: CSU, Sacramento Women's Resource Center.

Part 2

Hand out the story to students to read individually.

Part 3

Ask the students to answer the questions following the story in small groups. Bring the class together to discuss and clarify their answers.

Stages of Acquaintance Rape

▶ Intrusion: The rapist makes the victim feel uncomfortable with an unwanted touch or look. The rapist notices the victim's reaction and proceeds from there.

▶ Desensitization: The victim ignores the rapist's intrusions or makes excuses for them. She doesn't take the rapist seriously or thinks, *That's just the way he is.*

▶ Isolation: The rapist gets the victim alone, whether in a car, an apartment, or outside.

Overhead—*From J. Neide, 2009, Teaching Self-Defense in Secondary Physical Education (Champaign, IL: Human Kinetics).*

Scenario for Stages of Acquaintance Rape

Mike and Keri are college friends who previously dated casually. Keri is involved with someone else, but she and Mike are still friends. One night Keri's boyfriend is gone, and she and Mike go out for drinks. Mike keeps buying Keri drinks even after she says she has had enough. When Mike says that he's glad that Keri's boyfriend is out of town, she doesn't say anything. As Mike and Keri continue to drink, he puts his hand on her leg under the table. Keri feels uncomfortable, but she doesn't want to make a scene, so she ignores Mike's hand on her leg. As the night proceeds, Mike continues to get physically close to Keri. Keri jokes about having a boyfriend and how his hand on her leg and arm around her shoulder will get her into trouble, but she never says, "Stop."

Finally, they leave and Mike takes Keri home. He asks to come inside and Keri agrees. Mike then grabs her and pulls her toward the bedroom, saying that he just wants to hold her. Keri says she'd rather not, but he continues pulling her. Things get out of hand and Mike rapes Keri.

Questions

▸ When did the first intrusion take place?

▸ When was Keri desensitized?

▸ How did Keri become isolated?

From J. Neide, 2009, *Teaching Self-Defense in Secondary Physical Education* (Champaign, IL: Human Kinetics).

Legal Aspects of Self-Defense

Guilty or Not Guilty?

Focus

Students will examine the legal aspects of self-defense using an active learning strategy called a *jigsaw*. Each student in a group will focus on a different portion of the laws concerning self-defense, then share the information with the rest of the group. After the group members learn the combined material, they will complete the activity called You Be the Judge.

Objectives

Students will be able to do the following:

1. Define the terms *felony* and *misdemeanor*.
2. Summarize the basic legal aspects of self-defense.
3. Identify whether the defendant is guilty or not guilty by applying the legal aspects of self-defense.
4. Cooperate with their groups to complete the jigsaw activity.
5. Take responsibility for their learning.

Equipment and Facilities

- ▶ Gym
- ▶ Informational posters
- ▶ Masking tape
- ▶ Handout: You Be the Judge, page 123

Part 1

Create four posters with information on the legal aspects of self-defense (see teacher's resource), number them stations 1 to 4, and post them around the gym. Students will use the information on the posters to answer the questions on the handout.

Part 2

Ask the students to form into groups of four, and assign each member of the group a number from 1 to 4. Students are responsible for learning the information on the poster that corresponds to their assigned numbers, then share what they have learned with the group. In this way, the students learn the information on all four posters.

Part 3

Distribute the handout You Be the Judge to each group. Ask the students to answer the questions that follow each scenario using information from the posters. Students may return to the posters to review the material.

Part 4

After students have completed the handout, bring the class together to discuss their responses to each scenario. Give them the correct answers and explain any legal issues that might be unclear.

Teacher's Resource

Prepare individual station posters with the following information.

Station 1

Read and memorize the following information, and then return to your group.
Felony or Misdemeanor?

Most states divide their crimes into two major groups: felonies and misdemeanors. The classification of a crime depends on the severity of the potential punishment. If a law recommends imprisonment for longer than a year in response to a crime, it is usually considered a felony. If the potential punishment is for a year or less, then the act is considered a misdemeanor. In some states, certain crimes called *wobblers* exist that may be either a misdemeanor or a felony, because judges have the power to impose a sentence of less than a year or more than a year.

Behaviors punishable only by fine are usually not considered crimes at all, but infractions. Traffic tickets are an example. On occasion, legislatures may punish proven misdemeanors with only a fine. For example, possession of less than an ounce of marijuana for personal use could be considered an infraction in most states.

Station 2

Read and memorize the following information, and then return to your group.
Self-Defense

A defense to certain criminal charges involving force is called self defense. The basic rule is that if you are attacked or if a family member or friend is attacked, you can use any reasonable force needed to repel the aggressor. You can use greater force than your aggressor uses if your actions seem reasonable to you and you aren't held to a fine line deciding the difference.

You must use no more force than what is reasonably necessary for the circumstances. You will only be justified in using extreme force, likely to cause death or great bodily harm to your assailant, if you reasonably believe that you are in danger of death or great bodily harm.

Station 3

Read and memorize the following information, and then return to your group.
Self-Defense

You can use force to prevent an attack. If you feel threatened, you need not wait for an attack to use self-defense techniques. Even if you are mistaken, self-defense is justified if you genuinely believe that you are or another person is in present danger.

There are limits to how much force you can use on the streets. If possible, before striking a blow in self-defense, try to avoid violence by retreating. There is a fine line for legal self-defense if you have the opportunity to escape.

Verbal attacks call for restraint. You may not legally use physical force in response to profanity. If you react with force, you become the attacker.

Station 4

Read and memorize the following information, and then return to your group.
Self-Defense

The basic rule for self-defense in your home is that you don't need to retreat from an intruder, even if doing so would be reasonable and would prevent violence.

You may not use extreme violence against an unarmed person who enters your house to commit a larceny and does not threaten or act with the intention of hurting anyone if there are a number of people present who could easily secure the intruder.

If you cannot ascertain the intentions of the intruder, you may use any means against him, even taking his life.

You may not legally harm or use physical force against trespassers on the land outside your home unless they try to break into your home. You should try to chase the person away or call the police.

You Be the Judge

Read the following situations and determine if the characters are guilty or not guilty.

Scenario 1

Hank is new in school. Since the very first day, a group of boys has harassed him. In the beginning, the boys merely verbally harassed him, calling him names. However, now the situation has escalated and the group is threatening to physically hurt Hank.

After school, Hank goes to his car in the parking lot and finds that the sides of his car have been scratched by a set of keys. A group of boys watching him from a distance begins to laugh. Hank runs toward the group, tackles a boy in the group named Joe, and tries to restrain him. Hank yells for help. Joe fights back, but Hank hits him hard enough to keep him from running away until the police come. Joe is taken to the hospital with a broken jaw and Hank is taken to the police station.

Questions

1. Who is guilty of assault, Joe or Hank?
2. Is the assault justifiable?
3. How do you think each crime (vandalism and assault) will be classified: infraction, misdemeanor, or felony?

Scenario 2

Loren, 18 years old, has been asked to stay with her grandmother for the weekend. Her grandmother has been sick and needs someone to monitor her medication. Loren's parents ask her to be very careful and give her pepper spray for protection.

During the night while Loren is staying at her grandmother's house, she hears a noise in the kitchen. She feels afraid and unsafe, so she takes the pepper spray and goes into the kitchen. A man is looking through the kitchen drawers. When he hears Loren in the kitchen, he immediately moves toward the back door and shouts that he does not want to hurt her. Loren makes the decision to use the pepper spray because she is not sure of his intentions. The man grabs his eyes, stumbles out the door, and falls down the stairs. He breaks his leg during the fall. Loren calls the police.

Questions

1. Is the man guilty of larceny?
2. Is the man guilty of breaking and entering?
3. Is Loren justified in using the pepper spray?
4. Can Loren be charged with assault?

From J. Neide, 2009, Teaching Self-Defense in Secondary Physical Education (Champaign, IL: Human Kinetics).

Knowing Your Rights
and Trusting Your Feelings

Focus

Panel on dating: Knowing your rights and trusting your feelings.

Objectives

Students will be able to discuss and analyze issues concerning dating, rights, and how to trust their feelings.

Equipment and Facilities

▶ Gym

▶ Six chairs for panel

Part 1

1. Select an issue concerning dating that will engage students' interest (see teacher's resource for sample issues). Present the issue in a way that stimulates students to discuss their views. Identify questions for the selected issue.

2. Choose six students (three boys and three girls) to serve as a panel discussion group. Arrange chairs for them in a semicircle at the front of the room.

3. Ask the class to arrange their chairs around the panel group in a horseshoe shape.

4. Begin with a provocative opening question. Moderate a discussion between the panel and the core group. Ask the core group to think of questions to ask the panel. Emphasize how our perceptions of gender roles affect our responses to the questions.

5. At the end of the designated discussion period, allow the class to ask you questions.

6. Allow time for the class to divide into small groups and continue the discussion.

Variations

Reverse the sequence by beginning with small group discussion, then moving to a panel discussion.

Teacher's Resource

Dating

Issue: If someone asks you out, you are obligated to go on the date.

  a. Does a girl or boy have the right to turn down a date?

  b. What are appropriate ways to refuse a date?

Issue: If a girl is on a date, she should not express an opinion on which movie they will see because the boy is paying for everything.

  a. Does a girl have the right to express her opinion on which movie they should see?

  b. How should they decide which movie to see?

Issue: After a date, the girl is obligated to kiss the boy good night.

  a. Does a girl have to kiss her date good night?
  b. What are some good strategies that a girl can use if she doesn't want to kiss after a date?

Issue: All boys must present themselves as strong and aggressive.

  a. What is your reaction to a boy who begins crying during a sad portion of a movie?
  b. Why is it acceptable for a girl to show emotion, but not a boy?

Issue: You cannot go to a school dance by yourself.

  a. How would your friends react if you went to a dance by yourself?

Issue: Girls must wear the current fashions at all times, but boys can wear anything they want.

  a. How important is clothing to your popularity?
  b. Are girls asking for it if they wear very revealing outfits?

Issue: Demeaning words toward girls don't really hurt anyone or mean anything.

  a. Do the words and messages in current music really mean anything?
  b. Are the lyrics criticizing and demeaning women?

Issue: When boys check out and rate girls, it is only a game. It doesn't mean anything.

  a. Do boys really only look at the outside, not caring what the person is actually like?
  b. Is this true for girls too?
  c. When someone checks you out, how do you feel?

Part 2

Summarize the key points of gender stereotyping (see Acquaintance Rape and Gender Stereotyping, page 113). You should emphasize that students must trust any feelings of discomfort when dating, and that anyone has the right to say no.

Appendix

Self-Defense Final Exam

(25 points)

Please answer the following questions. Mark your response on the answer sheet. Each question has only one correct answer.

1. If you are in immediate bodily danger, which two areas of the assailant's body should you strike first?

   a. knee and abdomen

   b. knee and chin

   c. eyes and abdomen

   d. eyes and groin

2. What should be your first reaction if you receive an obscene phone call?

   a. Hang up immediately.

   b. Ask who is calling.

   c. Listen quietly to discover who is calling.

   d. Scream at the caller, "Stop calling or I will call the police!"

3. You are shopping by yourself and you think you are being followed. What should you do?

   a. Find a restroom immediately, go inside, and hide.

   b. Run to your car and lock yourself in.

   c. Go into a store and tell a store clerk you think you are being followed.

   d. Ignore the person until he or she goes away.

4. For a crime to occur, the following factors must be present: desire, ability, and opportunity.

   a. true

   b. false

5. Dead bolts provide more protection and deter burglars more than other door locks.

   a. true

   b. false

6. A good way to prevent a burglar from getting into a window is to

   a. plant flowers in front of the window

   b. pile garbage bins in front of the window

   c. install safety locks on all windows

   d. keep only the top of the window open

7. Families should never use metal bars on the windows unless

   a. the metal bars can be opened from inside the house during a fire

   b. the metal bars are electrified

   c. all the small children in the home know how to exit through the front door during a fire

   d. they keep a dog in the home

8. When you are sleeping, it is best to leave a light on in which room?

   a. garage

   b. dining room

   c. kitchen

   d. bathroom

(continued)

From J. Neide, 2009, *Teaching Self-Defense in Secondary Physical Education* (Champaign, IL: Human Kinetics).

9. If you come home and you believe someone has broken into the house, you should enter immediately to make sure nothing has been stolen.
    a. true
    b. false

10. When you are walking alone, it is advisable to walk
    a. with traffic
    b. against traffic

11. It is okay to give personal information over the phone to a salesperson.
    a. true
    b. false

12. It is not necessary to report a suspicious person on your street. Anyone is allowed to walk on a public street.
    a. true
    b. false

13. Accepting a ride from a stranger is okay during the day, but never at night.
    a. true
    b. false

14. You can deescalate a potential assault by
    a. threatening the attacker
    b. staying calm, but alert
    c. ignoring the person
    d. getting close to the potential attacker's face and staring

15. Which behaviors characterize a defensive stance?
    a. Stand tall and face the assailant straight on.
    b. Turn your back to the assailant and get ready to run.
    c. Crouch low to the ground, hold your arms down, and be assertive.
    d. Angle the side of your body toward the potential assailant, hold your arms up, and bend your knees.

16. If a crime is punishable with imprisonment for less than a year, it is considered a
    a. misdemeanor
    b. felony

17. It is legal to use any type of force at any time, even a gun, to stop a crime.
    a. true
    b. false

18. You should never run away from an assailant. It is better to fight than to run.
    a. true
    b. false

19. When you execute a punch or kick, delivering a loud yell at the moment of impact can help you feel physically and psychologically strong.
    a. true
    b. false

(continued)

20. When you deliver a front punch, you should make contact with the
    a. top two knuckles
    b. thumb
    c. little finger
    d. wrist

21. When you deliver a heel-of-palm strike, you should aim at the assailant's
    a. abdomen
    b. knee
    c. nose or chin
    d. ear

22. When practicing or drilling self-defense techniques, you should always use full speed and maximum force. It is your partner's job to stay safe.
    a. true
    b. false

23. When your life is in danger, you should *never* use force. Instead, try to talk your way out of the situation.
    a. true
    b. false

24. When an attacker is about to choke you, it is best to stay calm and hope that he or she stops.
    a. true
    b. false

25. In self-defense, you should try to avoid conflict before fighting back.
    a. true
    b. false

From J. Neide, 2009, *Teaching Self-Defense in Secondary Physical Education* (Champaign, IL: Human Kinetics).

Final Exam Answer Sheet

1.	d	14.	b
2.	a	15.	d
3.	c	16.	a
4.	a	17.	b
5.	a	18.	b
6.	c	19.	a
7.	a	20.	a
8.	d	21.	c
9.	b	22.	b
10.	b	23.	b
11.	b	24.	b
12.	b	25.	a
13.	b		

From J. Neide, 2009, Teaching Self-Defense in Secondary Physical Education (Champaign, IL: Human Kinetics).

Homework Ideas

Home and Personal Safety

Complete the following questions:

1. How can you protect your home when you leave for a day or longer?
2. What do you do if an intruder comes while you are away?
3. What do you do if an intruder comes while you are in the house?
4. How can you protect yourself from phone scams and unwanted calls?
5. How can you protect yourself from unwanted attention in chat rooms on the Internet?

List preventive safety advice for the following situations:

1. Walking
2. Using public transportation
3. Using a car
4. Encountering harassment
5. Walking in school hallways

Fears and Apprehensions

Part 1

Write a paper describing your fears and apprehensions concerning your personal safety. This might include, but is not limited to, fears about the following:

▶ Safety at home or at work
▶ Safety in places that you frequent
▶ Relationships with people
▶ Using a car or public transportation

Part 2

After you complete the assignment from part 1, please develop a strategy to eliminate or minimize one of your fears. Write out the steps for your strategy.

Crime Statistics

On the Internet, look up the crime statistics for your neighborhood. Report your findings by answering the following questions: who, what, when, where, and how?

Text Review

Read a text that focuses on personal self-defense and write a review. Your review can include, but is not limited to, the following topics:

Describe aspects of the text that were interesting to you.

Discuss points you agreed or disagreed with.

Discuss elements of the text that surprised you.

Which ideas from the text would you like to know more about?

(continued)

From J. Neide, 2009, Teaching Self-Defense in Secondary Physical Education (Champaign, IL: Human Kinetics).

Gender Stereotyping

Find an advertisement in a teen or fashion magazine that uses gender stereotypes. How do advertisements perpetuate the myth that women are weak and men are dominant? How do they perpetuate the myth that women are sex objects?

Write a concise paper that describes your chosen advertisement and your reaction to the preceding questions.

From J. Neide, 2009, Teaching Self-Defense in Secondary Physical Education (Champaign, IL: Human Kinetics).

About the Author

Joan Neide, EdD, is a professor of physical education at California State University at Sacramento, where she specializes in physical education pedagogy, history, and curriculum design. Dr. Neide earned her renshi (master instructor) rank in Uechi-ryu karate in 2002 and has taught self-defense for more than 30 years at the public school and university levels. She holds a seventh-degree black belt in Uechi-ryu karate and has combined her interestes in physical education and Asian studies to include research in Southeast Asian children's play patterns as well as the study of martial arts.

TEACHING SELF-DEFENSE IN SECONDARY PHYSICAL EDUCATION DVD ORDER FORM

To purchase the DVD titled *Teaching Self-Defense in Secondary Physical Education* to accompany this textbook, please contact the Hornet Bookstore at California State University, Sacramento.

Hornet Bookstore
Textbook Department
6000 J Street
Sacramento, CA 95819
Phone: 916-278-6445
Fax: 916-278-5287

You may also purchase this DVD online. For convenient and secure online ordering, go to www.hornetbookstore.com. A credit card is required for online ordering. Select "Textbooks," choose "CCE," choose any term, select "Your Department," and select "Neide DVD." Please contact the Hornet Bookstore at the phone number above if you have any questions.